总 策 划：许　琳

总 监 制：夏建辉　王君校

监　　制：韩　晖　张彤辉　顾　蕾　刘根芹


主　　编：吴中伟

编　　者：吴中伟　吴叔平　高顺全　吴金利

修　　订：吴中伟

顾　　问：陶黎铭　陈光磊

Dāngdài Zhōngwén

# 当代中文

## 修订版

# Contemporary Chinese
## Revised Edition

Kèběn

# 课本
## 2

# TEXTBOOK
## Volume Two

主　编：吴中伟

编　者：吴中伟　吴叔平

　　　　高顺全　吴金利

翻　译：徐　蔚

　　　　Yvonne L. Walls　Jan W. Walls

译文审校：Jerry Schmidt

华语教学出版社
SINOLINGUA

First Edition  2003

Revised Edition  2015

Sixth Printing  2020

ISBN 978-7-5138-0731-9

Copyright 2014 by Confucius Institute Headquarters (Hanban)

Published by Sinolingua Co., Ltd

24 Baiwanzhuang Road, Beijing 100037, China

Tel: (86)10-68320585, 68997826

Fax: (86)10-68997826, 68326333

http://www.sinolingua.com.cn

E-mail: hyjx@sinolingua.com.cn

Facebook: www.facebook.com/sinolingua

Printed by Beijing Mixing Printing Co., Ltd.

*Printed in the People's Republic of China*

# User's Guide to the Revised Edition

The Chinese language learning course book series *Contemporary Chinese* is designed around the basis of grammatical structure and is integrated with differing topics, functions and cultural aspects. This series is aimed at developing students' comprehensive skills of listening to, speaking, reading and writing Chinese. It includes *Textbook* volumes one through four, with an accompanying *Exercise Book* and *Teacher's Book* for each, audio materials as well as a *Character Book* for Volume 1 and Volume 2.

The first edition of *Contemporary Chinese* was published in 2003. The series is now in its revised edition and has been modified based on suggestions from readers worldwide and taking into consideration the Chinese Proficiency Test Syllabus and the International Curriculum for Chinese Language Education. This edition retains many features from the first edition, with some mistakes corrected and part of the texts updated. Some exercises and activities have been added in the *Textbook* while *Testing Materials* and *Supplementary Reading Materials* will be offered for this edition.

Features of this series:

1. Elementary-level instruction: Equal importance should be attached to conversation, phonetics and Chinese characters, and a systematic approach should be taken to teach these three aspects independently. Phonetics is the key to speech and thus will become the teaching focus at the elementary level; while Chinese characters are the stepping stone to reading and writing, characters should be taught beginning with basic strokes and stroke orders and a few characters with typical structures so as to cultivate a sense of their overall structure in students. Conversation should be taught by asking students to repeat full sentences after listening. We suggest that 1/5 of a class period be spent in teaching conversation, 3/5 training phonetics and 1/5 practicing characters successively so that this course will not only help students to create a solid foundation of phonetics and Chinese characters, but also satisfy their communication desire, break the normal learning routine and help them to acquire a sense of achievement.

2. Phonetic instruction: At the elementary-level, phonetic teaching should be carried out from an overview of the subject to details, then back to an overview. In this way, students can, at the outset, obtain a full picture of Chinese phonetics, then a focus may be put on training students' pronunciation step by step, then finally having the students review what they have learned. Despite all the phonemes being listed in the textbook, a concentration on teaching difficult phonemes should be made instead of putting equal focus on all. Translations are given for corresponding pinyin vocabulary words so as to reduce the monotony of memorizing meaningless phonetic units. The textbook combines the teaching of syllables and phonemes with that of speech flow. Instruction may begin from syllable to phoneme so as to improve accuracy of the latter, or from syllable to speech flow so as to reveal the functions and changes of phonetics during vernacular discourse. Phonetic teaching is a long-term task; therefore, phonetic training remains a major part of the textbook after the elementary level.

3. Chinese character instruction: The *Character Book,* for volumes 1 and 2 of the textbook series, is designed based on the unique features of Chinese characters to improve teaching effectiveness. In the series we will shift from the traditional method of requiring students to recognize and write characters simultaneously to the method of separating the two processes; first reading, and later writing at the elementary level. After the elementary level, we will continue to distinguish these two processes by only requiring students to be able to read and write around 25 characters per unit. By the end of Volume 2, students will possess the competence to simultaneously read and write Chinese characters. At this stage, character exercises need to be strengthened while stories related to characters can be told so as to stimulate students' interest in learning and help them to better memorize and understand Chinese.

4. Vocabulary instruction: The vocabulary in this series can be used independently of other segments. They are organized in a practical and systematic way with special exercises designed around them. The words in the glossaries of volumes 1 and 2 are arranged based on the intrinsic meaning of or grammatical functions between words instead of their order of appearance in the text. Some of the words in the glossary do not appear in text. For example, only the character 女 appears in the text, but the glossary will contain both 女 and 男. In addition, the course book series places a premium on the instruction of morphemes and adopts the teaching method of combining characters into words or associating words with characters. In *Character Book*, the meaning of morphemes for certain words is presented and then combined with previously learned char-

acters to form new words so as to expand students' vocabulary.

5. Grammar instruction: This series keeps the grammar to the simplest level, and focuses on the application of grammar and the learning habits of non-native learners. One approach adopted is to treat grammar points as the usages of words or phrases. For instance, the series does not list the modal verb as a grammar point as in its earlier edition. Instead, the similarities and differences between two modal verbs 能 and 会 are introduced. Another approach is to bypass some grammar points such as complex sentences and introduce correlatives as new words such as 可是 and 所以 at an early stage. Students will learn the new words first and the grammar later. The grammar points included in the book are sequenced according to their levels of difficulty and are reinforced at various stages. Many exercises are provided to train students' ability to translate the grammatical knowledge into a functional command of the language. Grammar terms are kept at a minimal level and more semantic and pragmatic explanations are provided. More detailed grammar points and some grammar related questions are included in the *Teacher's Book* for the benefit of the teachers.

6. Culture instruction: This series emphasizes everyday life, trends of the current age and contemporary issues, and features cultural differences and common grounds to make Chinese more relatable to students. The texts combine information about China and learners' native countries, with a focus on the former. Traditional culture and contemporary society are both covered, with a focus on the latter.

7. Exercises and activities: *Textbook* is composed of different units. In volumes 1 and 2, each unit is divided into three parts. Texts are the core of the first two parts and each text is preceded by certain warm-up activities, vocabulary exercises as well as grammar exercises. Such a scaffolding of activities and exercises are a manifestation of the teaching process aimed at examining students' preview of the vocabulary and familiarizing them with words and expressions as well as key grammar points. Furthermore, each text is followed by corresponding questions designed to check students' understanding along with certain extension tasks so as to cater to the various needs of students, which makes the series more adaptable to individual users. Language points and cultural notes constitute the third part of each unit. Cultural notes are provided for general reading while language points can be seen as a summary of the unit's key teaching points. These language points should be integrated into the course lesson plans; teachers can also use these language points to give error correcting feedback to students through the exercises.

The *Exercise Book* supplements the *Textbook*. The listening and reading exercises in the *Exercise Book* are designed to include some new words. Students are not expected to learn them as they will not affect their ability to answer the questions. This arrangement allows students to familiarize themselves with authentic communication scenarios and enhance their ability to communicate with the Chinese people in real life.

8. Teaching plans: Each volume of this series is divided into 12 units and it is suggested that 6-8 class periods be spent on each unit (Volume 1 contains eight units preceded by Unit 0, which is a preparation unit that can be covered over 24 class periods). Thus, each volume will take one semester or a school year to complete depending on the weekly class hour arrangement of the course and the level of students.

For more information regarding the basic structure and compiling thought of the series, as well as other reference materials, background information and teaching advice, please refer to the *Teacher's Book*.

We are always grateful for any of your suggestions and advice.

Wu Zhongwei
wuzhongwei@fudan.edu.cn

# To the Learner

**Welcome to *Contemporary Chinese*!**

*Contemporary Chinese* is designed for students whose native language is English. The ultimate goal of this series is to develop the student's ability to comprehend and communicate in the Chinese language. Specifically, it provides training in the skills of listening to, speaking, reading, and writing Chinese.

The whole series consists of **four volumes**. You may work through the whole series or use only the volumes of your choice.

The following are to be used together with the **Textbook**:

* **Exercise Book**

* **Character Book (only for Volume One and Volume Two)**

* **Audio materials and CD-ROM**

* **Teacher's Book**

* **Testing Materials**

* **Supplementary Reading Materials**


The **Textbook**:

➢ is concise, practical, authentic, and topical,

➢ is adaptable to the varied needs of different students,

➢ gives equal attention to listening, speaking, reading, and writing,

➢ guides your learning step by step.


After working through Volume Two, you should have a good command of 472 new Chinese words and expressions, 316 new Chinese characters, 27 new grammar items, and 44 new communicative function items. Together with the 337 Chinese words and expressions, 317 Chinese characters, 27 grammar items, and 23 communicative function items in Volume One, you will feel much more free to communicate in Chinese now.

## Greetings and Polite Expressions

| | | |
|---|---|---|
| 你好！ | Nǐ hǎo! | Hello! |
| 你好！ | Nǐ hǎo! | Hello! |
| 谢谢！ | Xièxie! | Thank you! |
| 不客气。 | Bú kèqi. | You are welcome. |
| 对不起！ | Duìbuqǐ! | I'm sorry. |
| 没关系。 | Méi guānxi. | That's all right. |
| 再见！ | Zàijiàn! | Goodbye! |
| 再见！ | Zàijiàn! | Goodbye! |

Shàng kè.                                   Class begins.

Xià kè.                                      Class is over.

Xiànzài xiūxi yíxià.                         Now let's have a rest.

Xiànzài jìxù shàng kè.                       Now let's continue.


Qǐng dǎkāi shū, fāndào dì-sān yè.            Open your books and turn to page 3, please.

Qǐng tīng lùyīn.                             Listen to the recording, please.

Qǐng gēn wǒ dú.                              Read after me, please.

Qǐng zài shuō yí biàn.                       Say it again, please.


Zhè shì shénme yìsi?                         What does this mean?

··· (Hànyǔ) zěnme shuō?                      How do you say … in Chinese?

··· (Hànzì) zěnme xiě?                       How do you write …?


Qǐng dú yíxià.                               Read it, please.

Qǐng xiě yíxià.                              Write it, please.

Qǐng fānyì yíxià.                            Translate it, please.


Duì bu duì?                                   Is it right?

Duì.                                         Yes, it is. / It's right.

Bú duì.                                      No, it isn't. / It's not right.


Qǐng kàn hēibǎn.                             Look at the blackboard, please.

Xiànzài tīngxiě.                             Let's have a dictation now.

Xiànzài zuò liànxí.                          Let's do exercises now.

Jīntiān de zuòyè shì ···                     Today's homework is …

# Chinese Grammar Terms

| | | | |
|---|---|---|---|
| noun | N. | míngcí | 名词 |
| place word | PW | chùsuǒcí | 处所词 |
| time word | TW | shíjiāncí | 时间词 |
| location word | LW | fāngwèicí | 方位词 |
| pronoun | Pron. | dàicí | 代词 |
| question word | QW | yíwèncí | 疑问词 |
| verb | V. | dòngcí | 动词 |
| directional verb | DV | qūxiàng dòngcí | 趋向动词 |
| modal verb | MV | néngyuàn dòngcí | 能愿动词 |
| adjective | Adj. | xíngróngcí | 形容词 |
| numeral | Num. | shùcí | 数词 |
| measure word | MW | liàngcí | 量词 |
| adverb | Adv. | fùcí | 副词 |
| preposition | Prep. | jiècí | 介词 |
| conjunction | Conj. | liáncí | 连词 |
| particle | Part. | zhùcí | 助词 |
| interjection | Interj. | tàncí | 叹词 |
| subject | Subj. | zhǔyǔ | 主语 |
| predicate | Pred. | wèiyǔ | 谓语 |
| object | Obj. | bīnyǔ | 宾语 |
| attributive | Attrib. | dìngyǔ | 定语 |
| complement | Comple. | bǔyǔ | 补语 |
| adverbial | Adverbial | zhuàngyǔ | 状语 |

There is a famous university named Lincoln University, in a beautiful city on the west coast of North America. Young people from different countries study there:

Bái Xiǎohóng

白小红
female, Chinese

Wáng Yīng

王 英 female,
Chinese
-Canadian

Jiāng Shān

江山
male, American

Mǎdīng

马丁
male, Australian

There are several friends who work in companies; and one more, currently in the U.K. They soon got to know a group of Chinese friends:

Dīng Hànshēng

丁汉生 male, Chinese, who was sent to work here by a Chinese company.

Jiékè

杰克 Jack, male, Canadian, who is an employee of an export company and often goes to China on business.

Zhāng Yuányuan

张园园 female, English of Chinese origin, Jiang Shan's girl friend, a student at the Eastern College in England.

Lǐqí

里奇
American male.

They have a Chinese teacher who always pretends not to know English when in the class:

Zhāng Lín
张林
male, Chinese, over forty.

Tiánzhōng
田中 Japanese
female.

Jīn Róngnán
金容南 South Korean
female.

Gāo Yīfēi
高一飞 Chinese male,
a university graduate
student.

Xiǎo Zhāng
小 张 Chinese
female, a univer-
sity undergraduate
student, Liqi's
girlfriend.

Lǐ Xiǎoyǔ
李小雨 Chinese female, an
employee of a joint-venture
company, Ma Li's colleague and
language partner, later married to
Ma Li.

Chén Jìng
陈 静 Chinese female, Jack's
language partner.

# Unit 1

## Nǐ Dēngguo Chángchéng Ma?
## 你 登 过 长城 吗？
## Have You Ever Climbed the Great Wall?

### Learning objectives

* Expressing past experiences
* Expressing new changes and recent plans
* Discussing one's likes and dislikes
* Pets
* Tourist attractions in China

### Key sentences

Wǒ yǐqián yǎngguo niǎor.
我 以前 养 过 鸟儿。
I've raised birds before.

Nǐ duì Běijīng hěn shúxi le ba.
你 对 北京 很 熟悉 了吧。
You must be very familiar with Beijing by now.

Tīngshuō， nǐ yào qù Běijīng le?
听说 ，你 要 去 北京 了？
I heard that you're going to Beijing. Is it true?

Nǐ yě xǐhuan yǎng xiǎo dòngwù?
你 也 喜欢 养 小 动物？
Do you like raising small animals, too?

Yàoshi nǐ xiǎng qù dehuà，wǒ péi nǐ yìqǐ qù.
要是 你 想 去 的话 ，我 陪 你 一起 去。
If you want to go, I can accompany you.

# 1.1 Wǒ Yǐqián Yǎngguo Niǎor
# 我 以前 养过 鸟儿
# I've raised birds before

## Preliminary exercises

**1 Warm up**

你喜欢养宠物 (chǒngwù, pet) 吗？为什么？

你知道中国人喜欢在家里养一些什么东西吗？

**2 Learn the following words and form correct sentences with the words under the teacher's guidance.**

（1）小动物　他　喜欢　非常

（2）狗和猫　他　喜欢　不　都

（3）麻烦　养　花儿　太　了

（4）事儿　的　他　自己　这　是，让　做　他　自己　吧

（5）对不起，我　你　见面　跟　没有　时间　今天

（6）养　狗　喜欢　有的　人，养　猫　喜欢　有的　人，
　　养　花儿　喜欢　有的　人　还

**3 Listen to the recording and fill in 过 or 了 in the blanks.**

（1）我以前不会说汉语，现在会说______。

（2）他以前养______几只小动物，现在没有时间______，不养______。

（3）他以前在北京工作______，所以会说一点儿北京话。

（4）我以前没来______这儿，这是第一次来。

Question:

What do 了 and 过 mean, respectively, in the sentences above?

**Listening script**

3（1）我以前不会说汉语，现在会说了。

（2）他以前养过几只小动物，现在没有时间了，不养了。

（3）他以前在北京工作过，所以会说一点儿北京话。

（4）我以前没来过这儿，这是第一次来。

## Words and expressions

| 1. | 养 | ( V. ) | yǎng | raise (animals), grow (flowers), etc. |
| 2. | 动物 | ( N. ) | dòngwù | animal |
| 3. | 狗 | ( N. ) | gǒu | dog |
| 4. | 猫 | ( N. ) | māo | cat |
| 5. | 鸟儿 | ( N. ) | niǎor | bird |
| 6. | 只 | ( MW ) | zhī | a measure word for birds, cats, little dogs, etc. |
| 7. | 花儿 | ( N. ) | huār | flower |
| 8. | 城市 | ( N. ) | chéngshì | city |
| 9. | 时间 | ( N. ) | shíjiān | time |
| 10. | 老人家 | ( N. ) | lǎorénjia | Sir/Madam (for elderly people) |
| 11. | 自己 | ( Pron. ) | zìjǐ | oneself |
| 12. | 有的 | ( Pron. ) | yǒude | some |
| 13. | 听说 | ( V. ) | tīngshuō | it is said; to hear tell of something |
| 14. | 麻烦 | ( Adj. & V. & N. ) | máfan | troublesome；(to) trouble |
| 15. | 但是 | ( Conj. ) | dànshì | but |
| 16. | 所以 | ( Conj. ) | suǒyǐ | so, therefore |
| 17. | 过 | ( Part. ) | guo | used after a verb to indicate the completion of an action |
| 18. | 了 | ( Part. ) | le | used to indicate a change of situation or state |

✿ Listen to the dialogue and answer the following questions in Chinese.

（1）老人家以前养过什么？现在养什么？

（2）在中国也有人养狗吗？还养什么？

（3）江山喜欢不喜欢小动物？他养不养小动物？为什么？

✿ Listen to the recording while reading the text on the next page.

✿ Read the text aloud and try not to look at the pinyin.

✿ Work in groups and act out the conversation.

✿ Activity

Students: What pets do/did you have?

**Vocabulary extension**

| | | | | | | |
|---|---|---|---|---|---|---|
| 宠物 | chǒngwù | pet | 兔子 | tùzi | rabbit |
| 乌龟 | wūguī | tortoise | 金鱼 | jīnyú | goldfish |
| 松鼠 | sōngshǔ | squirrel | 遛狗 | liù gǒu | walk the dog |
| 好养 | hǎo yǎng | easy to raise | 不好养 | bù hǎo yǎng | not eay to raise |
| 死 | sǐ | to die; dead | 活 | huó | to live (as opposed to 死) |

_____    _____

_____    _____

(On the eastern shores of the Pacific Ocean, Jiang Shan and the others are still studying at college; their Chinese is getting better and better. Today, Jiang Shan is going to see Ding Hansheng. Right now he is chatting with Ding Hansheng's father.)

Jiāng Shān: Lǎorén jia, zhè zhī xiǎo gǒu zhēn kě'ài.
江　山：老人家，这只小狗真可爱。 *starting a conversation*

Lǎorén: Shì a. Wǒ yǐqián yǎngguo huār, yǎngguo niǎor, dànshì bù
老　人：是啊。我以前养过花儿，养过鸟儿，但是不

xǐhuan yǎng gǒu. Lái zhèr yǐhòu, zhèr de rén dōu xǐhuan
喜欢养狗。来这儿以后，这儿的人都喜欢

yǎng gǒu, wǒ yě yǎng gǒu le.
养狗，我也养狗了。

Jiāng Shān: Tīngshuō zài Zhōngguó chéngshì li bù néng yǎng gǒu, shì ma?
江　山：听说在中国城市里不能养狗，是吗？

Lǎorén: Yǐqián bù xíng, xiànzài kěyǐ le. Yǒude rén xǐhuan yǎng gǒu,
老　人：以前不行，现在可以了。有的人喜欢养狗，

yǒude rén xǐhuan yǎng māo, yǒude rén xǐhuan yǎng niǎor, hái yǒude
有的人喜欢养猫，有的人喜欢养鸟儿，还有的

rén xǐhuan yǎng yú … Nǐ yě xǐhuan yǎng xiǎo dòngwù?
人喜欢养鱼……你也喜欢养小动物？ *likes and dislikes*

Jiāng Shān: Wǒ xǐhuan xiǎo dòngwù, dànshì bù yǎng xiǎo dòngwù.
江　山：我喜欢小动物，但是不养小动物。

Lǎorén: Wèi shénme? Shì bu shì tài máfan?
老　人：为什么？是不是太麻烦？

Jiāng Shān: Bú shì. Yīnwèi wǒ méiyǒu shíjiān, yě méiyǒu qián.
江　山：不是。因为我没有时间，也没有钱。

# 1.2

Nǐ Duì Běijīng Hěn Shúxi Le Ba?

## 你 对 北京 很 熟悉了吧?

## You must be very familiar with Beijing by now?

---

### Preliminary exercises

**1 Warm up**

你去过北京吗?

北京有哪些好玩儿的地方,你知道吗?

**2 Learn the following words and form correct sentences with the words under the teacher's guidance.**

(1)登 他 喜欢 山

(2)有意思 照片 这些 都 非常

(3)城市 这 个 我 熟悉 对 不太

(4)没有 飞机 那儿,坐 得 你 火车

(5)你看,麻烦 现在 有了, 办 怎么 打算 你

(6)要是 的话 有空 你, 能不能 陪 去 买 东西 我

**3 Add 了 to the following sentences according to the recording.**

(1)我们快要放假_____。

(2)她下个星期就要回国_____。

(3)你现在可以进来_____。

(4)他孩子不见_____!

Question:

What do the above sentences mean? How many usages of 了 were employed in the above sentences?

**Listening script**

3 (1)我们快要放假了。

(2)她下个星期就要回国了。

(3)你现在可以进来了。

(4)他孩子不见了!

**Words and expressions**

| | | | | |
|---|---|---|---|---|
| 1. | 办 | ( V. ) | bàn | do, handle, manage |
| 2. | 陪 | ( V. ) | péi | accompany |
| 3. | 登 | ( V. ) | dēng | climb (a mountain, a high top) |
| 4. | 不到长城非好汉 | | bú dào Chángchéng fēi hǎohàn | You're not a true man if you haven't conquered the Great Wall. |
| | 非 | | fēi | not |
| | 好汉 | ( N. ) | hǎohàn | brave man; true man |
| 5. | 得 | ( MV ) | děi | have to; must |
| 6. | 对……熟悉 | | duì … shúxi | be familiar with … |
| | 对 | ( Prep. ) | duì | to, with |
| | 熟悉 | ( V. ) | shúxi | be familiar with … |
| 7. | 欢迎 | ( V. ) | huānyíng | welcome |
| 8. | 照片 | ( N. ) | zhàopiàn | photo |
| 9. | 拍照 | ( V.O.) | pāizhào | take photos |
| 10. | 别的 | ( Pron. ) | biéde | other |
| 11. | 别人 | ( Pron. ) | biéren | other people |
| 12. | 要是……的话 | | yàoshi … dehuà | if |
| | 要是 | ( Conj. ) | yàoshi | if |
| | ……的话 | | … dehuà | if |
| 13. | （飞）机票 | | (fēi) jīpiào | plane ticket |
| | 飞机 | ( N. ) | fēijī | plane |
| | 票 | ( N. ) | piào | ticket |
| 14. | 火车 | ( N. ) | huǒchē | train |
| 15. | 些 | ( MW ) | xiē | some; a few; a little |
| | 这些 | | zhèxiē | these |
| | 那些 | | nàxiē | those |
| | 哪些 | | nǎxiē | which ones |
| | 一些 | | yìxiē | some |

## Proper nouns

| | | | |
|---|---|---|---|
| 1. | 故宫 | Gùgōng | the Palace Museum |

| 2. | 颐和园 | Yíhéyuán | the Summer Palace |
|----|--------|----------|-------------------|
| 3. | 长城 | Chángchéng | the Great Wall |
| 4. | 上海 | Shànghǎi | Shanghai |
| 5. | 西安 | Xī'ān | Xi'an |
| 6. | 成都 | Chéngdū | Chengdu |

☼ Listen to the dialogue and answer the following questions in Chinese.
（1）杰克什么时候去北京？他去北京旅游吗？
（2）杰克对北京熟悉不熟悉？
（3）杰克去过中国的哪些地方？他还想去哪儿？

☼ Listen to the recording while reading the text on the next page.

☼ Read the text aloud and try not to look at the pinyin.

☼ Work in groups and act out the conversation.

☼ Activity
Students: Where have you traveled? Do you want to visit these places again?

## Vocabulary extension

| 旅游 | lǚyóu | to tour | 出差 | chūchāi | go on a business trip |
|------|-------|---------|------|---------|------------------------|
| 景点 | jǐngdiǎn | scenic spots | 有名 | yǒumíng | famous |
| 照相 | zhàoxiàng | take photos | 照相机 | zhàoxiàngjī | camera |
| 如果 | rúguǒ | if | | | |

名胜古迹 míngshèng-gǔjì　famous scenic spots and historical sites

_____ 　 _____

_____ 　 _____

 **Text**

(Having just returned from China, Jack is going back to Beijing again, this time on business. He is saying goodbye to Bai Xiaohong.)

Bái Xiǎohóng: Tīngshuō, nǐ yào qù Běijīng le?
白小红：听说，你要去北京了？

> starting a conversation

Jiékè: Duì a, gōngsī ràng wǒ qù Běijīng bàn diǎnr shìr.
杰 克：对啊。公司让我去北京办点儿事儿。

Bái Xiǎohóng: Shénme shíhou zǒu?
白小红：什么时候走？

Jiékè: Xià xīngqīsān.
杰 克：下星期三。

Bái Xiǎohóng: Nǐ duì Běijīng hěn shúxi le ba?
白小红：你对北京很熟悉了吧？

Jiékè: Dāngrán. Nǐ kàn zhèxiē zhàopiàn. Zhè shì Gùgōng, zhè shì Yíhéyuán…
杰 克：当然。你看这些照片。这是故宫，这是颐和园……

Bái Xiǎohóng: Nǐ dēngguo Chángchéng ma?
白小红：你登过长城吗？

> talking about past experiences

Jiékè: "Bú dào Chángchéng fēi hǎohàn", wǒ zěnme néng bù dēng Chángchéng ne?
杰 克："不到长城非好汉"，我怎么能不登长城呢？

Bái Xiǎohóng: Nǐ hái qùguo biéde chéngshì ma?
白小红：你还去过别的城市吗？

Unit 1

杰　克：Jiékè: Shànghǎi, Xī'ān, Chéngdū... wǒ dōu qùguo. Kěshì, yǒu yí gè
上海、西安、成都……我都去过。可是，有一个

dìfang wǒ hái méi qùguo.
地方我还没去过。

白小红：Bái Xiǎohóng: Shénme dìfang?
白小红：什么地方？

杰　克：Jiékè: Nǐ de jiā.
杰　克：你的家。

白小红：Bái Xiǎohóng: Huānyíng nǐ qù ya! Yàoshi nǐ xiǎng qù dehuà, wǒ péi nǐ yìqǐ qù.
白小红：欢迎你去呀！要是你想去的话，我陪你一起去。

Dànshì, nǐ děi gěi wǒ mǎi jīpiào.
但是，你得给我买机票。

**offering a suggestion**

**making a request**

## 注释　Zhùshì　Notes

（一）要去北京了

要...了 indicates that an action is going to happen soon. Another example: 我们要放假了.

（二）我怎么能不登长城呢

This is a rhetorical question, which means 我当然要登长城.

## 1.3 Language Points

❖ I. The Particle 过 (guo) Indicating Past Experiences

The particle 过 follows a verb or an adjective to indicate that something has happened before. It is used to emphasize past experiences.

E.g. （1）他在北京住过，对北京很熟悉。
（2）我在那个饭店吃过中国菜，那儿的菜很好吃。

The negative form is expressed by adding 没（有）before the verb and keeping 过.

E.g. （1）他没去过北京，对北京不熟悉。
（2）我没吃过中国菜，不知道好吃不好吃。
（3）A：你知道他住哪儿吗？
　　　B：不知道。他没说过。

The interrogative form is: ... 吗？ / ... 没有 ？ / ...V. 没 V. 过 ...?

E.g. （1）你去过中国吗？
（2）你去过北京没有？
（3）你吃没吃过中国菜？

❖ II. The Particle 了 (le) Indicating Change of Situation

In the following sentences, the particle 了 is put at the end of a sentence to indicate that some change has occurred, or that a new situation has arisen.

E.g. （1）我以前每天看电视，现在忙了，没有时间看电视了。
（2）她今天有事儿，不能来上课了。
（3）九点了，我要回家了。

⚙ Complete the following sentences.

（1）我以前喜欢养狗，但是现在_____。（……了）
（2）他以前开车上班，但是从今年开始，他_____。（……了）
（3）听说你下个月_____，是真的吗？（要……了）
（4）这本书我以前_____，很不错，你也可以看看。（V 过）
（5）我不认识这个字，因为我们_____。　（没 V 过）
（6）明天晚上_____，我请你喝咖啡。（要是……的话）

1. China is a country rich in both natural scenery and cultural relics. Some examples are: the six ancient capitals—Beijing, Xi'an, Luoyang, Kaifeng, Nanjing, and Hangzhou; the great modern cities, such as Hong Kong, Shanghai, and Guangzhou; the scenery along the banks of the Yangtze River; the gardens of Suzhou; the tropical scenery of Southern China; the Confucian Temple at Qufu; cultural relics such as those found in the Dunhuang Grottoes on the ancient Silk Road; the natural scenery of the Gobi Desert; the Turpan Basin and the Flaming Mountains; the beautiful and ancient city of Lhasa; Buddhist temples throughout the country; the graceful Mount Huangshan, Mount Lushan, Mount Taishan, Lake Tai, the West Lake, the Lake of a Thousand Isles, and Sun Moon Lake. These sights, and many more, attract tourists from around the world.

\*　　　\*　　　\*

2. In China, many people, particularly the elderly, have the habit of exercising in the early morning in parks, athletic fields, or on lawns by the roadside. Many people also like to take their pet birds out in the early morning for fresh air and a chance to sing with the other birds.

If conditions permit, people like to grow flowers or raise birds, fish, cats, and dogs at home.

Even though more and more people like to raise dogs, the image of the dog in the Chinese language is usually not very flattering! It is very insulting to compare a person to a dog. In modern Chinese, most expressions containing the word "dog" are negative in connotation. For example:

(1) zǒugǒu: a lackey

(2) kānjiāgǒu: a dog kept to guard private property—someone who takes care of the affairs and property of his rich and powerful superior

(3) húpéng-gǒuyǒu: unsavory friends

(4) lángxīn-gǒufèi: rapacious as a wolf and savage as a cur; cruel and unscrupulous; ungrateful

(5) fànggǒupì: rubbish, nonsense, baloney

(6) tōujī-mōgǒu: to do something secretly, covertly

(7) gǒují-tiàoqiáng: when a dog is desperate, it will jump over a wall; a cornered animal or person will take desperate measures

(8) guà yángtóu mài gǒuròu: to display a sheep's head while actually selling dog meat; to sell something inferior to what is being advertised; the appearance is better than the content

(9) mài gǒupí gāoyào: literally, to sell dog skin plasters; to sell quack remedies

(10) gǒu zuǐ li tǔ bù chū xiàngyá: a dog's mouth can't produce ivory; a filthy mouth cannot utter decent words; we can't expect anything from a dog's mouth but a bark

(11) gǒu ná hàozi, duō guǎn xiánshì: a dog trying to catch mice; too meddlesome; poking one's nose into other people's business

# Unit 2

## Dàjiā Dōu Lái Le Ma?
## 大家 都 来 了 吗？
## Is Everyone Here?

## Learning objectives

✤ Expressing ongoing actions
✤ Completion of an action and the realization of an event
✤ Expressing speculations and estimations
✤ Body and health

### Key sentences

Xiànzài tā kěnéng zhèngzài chī zǎofàn.
现在 她 可能 正在 吃 早饭。
Maybe she is having breakfast now.

Wángyīng hái méi lái , biéde tóngxué dōu lái le.
王英 还 没 来，别的 同学 都 来了。
Wang Ying isn't here yet. The other students are all here.

Wángyīng qù yīyuàn le.
王英 去 医院 了。
Wang Ying went to the hospital.

Nǐ shì bu shì chīle bù gānjìng de dōngxi?
你 是 不 是 吃了 不 干净 的 东西？
Did you eat something bad?

Jīntiān zǎoshang wǒ chīle jǐ piàn miànbāo , hēle yì bēi niúnǎi.
今天 早上 我 吃了 几 片 面包，喝了 一杯 牛奶。
I had a few slices of bread and a glass of milk this morning.

# 2.1

Tā Qù Yīyuàn Le
## 她去医院了
## She went to the hospital

**↓ Preliminary exercises**

**1️⃣ Warm up**

要是今天班里有一位同学没来上课，请你用"可能"、"大概"或者"肯定"说一说他/她为什么没来。

**2️⃣ Learn the following words and form correct sentences with the words under the teacher's guidance.**

（1）住 他 宿舍 学生

（2）不好 很 迟到 上课

（3）舒服 不 有点儿 今天 他 身体

（4）病 你 了，陪 去 我 你 医院 吧

（5）在 学校 的 餐厅 吃 早饭 每 天 都 他

（6）睡觉 十一点 晚上 每天 他，起床 六点钟 早上

**3️⃣ Fill in the blanks according to the recording.**

（1）你＿＿＿＿＿＿＿干什么？我＿＿＿＿＿＿＿看书。

（2）昨天晚上你＿＿＿＿＿＿＿干什么？我＿＿＿＿＿＿＿看电视。

（3）小王在家吗？不在。他去公司＿＿＿＿＿＿＿。

（4）上课时间到＿＿＿＿＿＿＿，可是老师还＿＿＿＿＿＿＿来。

（5）他＿＿＿＿＿＿＿来＿＿＿＿＿＿＿，＿＿＿＿＿＿＿房间里等你呢！

Question:

In the above sentences, what do 在 , 正在 and 了 mean, respectively?

**Listening script**

（1）你在干什么？
我在看书。

（2）昨天晚上你在做什么？
我在看电视。

（3）小王在家吗？
不在，他去公司了。

（4）上课的时间到了，可是老师还没来。

（5）他已经来了，正在房间里等你呢！

**Words and expressions**

Unit
2

| 1. | 大家 | ( Pron. ) | dà jiā | everybody |
| 2. | 住 | ( V. ) | zhù | live |
| 3. | 宿舍 | ( N. ) | sùshè | dormitory |
| 4. | 天 / 日 | ( MW ) | tiān/rì | day |
| 5. | 餐厅 | ( N. ) | cāntīng | dining hall/room |
| 6. | 食堂 | ( N. ) | shítáng | dining hall; cafeteria |
| 7. | 早饭 | ( N. ) | zǎofàn | breakfast |
| 8. | 午饭 | ( N. ) | wǔfàn | lunch |
| 9. | 晚饭 | ( N. ) | wǎnfàn | supper |
| 10. | 睡觉 | ( V.O. ) | shuìjiào | sleep; go to bed |
| 11. | 起床 | ( V.O. ) | qǐchuáng | get up |
| | 起 | ( V. ) | qǐ | be up |
| | 床 | ( N. ) | chuáng | bed |
| 12. | 迟到 | ( V. ) | chídào | be late |
| 13. | 可能 | ( Adv. & Adj. ) | kěnéng | maybe, possible |
| 14. | 肯定 | ( Adj. ) | kěndìng | sure, certain |
| 15. | 错 | ( Adj. ) | cuò | wrong |
| 16. | 身体 | ( N. ) | shēntǐ | body, health |
| 17. | 舒服 | ( Adj. ) | shūfu | comfortable |
| 18. | 病 | ( V. & N. ) | bìng | be ill; sickness |
| 19. | 医院 | ( N. ) | yīyuàn | hospital |
| 20. | 正在 | ( Adv. ) | zhèngzài | key word for progressive actions |
| 21. | 在 | ( Adv. ) | zài | key word for progressive actions |
| 22. | 已经 | ( Adv. ) | yǐjīng | already (as opposed to "not yet") |
| 23. | 还 | ( Adv. ) | hái | still, yet |
| 24. | 没（有） | ( Adv. ) | méi (yǒu) | not |

⚙ Listen to the dialogue and answer the following questions in Chinese.

（1）同学们都来了没有？谁还没来？

（2）同学们说王英可能还在干什么？

（3）张园园告诉大家王英怎么了？

⚙ Listen to the recording while reading the text on the next page.

⚙ Read the text aloud and try not to look at the pinyin.

⚙ Work in groups and act out the conversation.

⚙ Activity

1. Guess "What did/will he do?": (1) Pick a day (yesterday, today, or tomorrow) and write down what you did/will do at that time on a piece of paper; (2) Make a guess at what your partner did/will do at that time; (3) Show your piece of paper to your partner and see whether he or she guessed the correct answer.

2. Guess "Where did he go?"/ "What did he do there?": (1) On a piece of paper, write down a time yesterday when you were not at home, also write down where you went or what you did; (2) Make a guess at where your partner went or what he or she did; (3) Show your piece of paper to your partner and see whether he or she guessed the correct answer.

## Vocabulary extension

| | | |
|---|---|---|
| 看报纸 | kàn bàozhǐ | read the newspaper |
| 运动 | yùndòng | sports; do physical exercises |
| 洗澡 | xǐzǎo | take a bath |
| 超市 | chāoshì | supermarket |
| 学生活动中心 | xuéshēng huódòng zhōngxīn | student activity center |
| 听音乐会 | tīng yīnyuèhuì | attend a concert |
| 听讲座 | tīng jiǎngzuò | attend a lecture |
| 看比赛 | kàn bǐsài | watch a match |
| 看电影 | kàn diànyǐng | see a movie |
| 聊天儿 | liáotiānr | to chat |
| 酒吧 | jiǔbā | bar |

**Text**

(This morning on the western shore of the Pacific Ocean, Martin and the others are in their college classroom. It's time for class, but Wang Ying isn't there yet.)

Lǎoshī: Dàjiā dōu lái le ma?
老 师：大家都来了吗？ [information]

Jiāng Shān: Wáng Yīng hái méi lái, biéde tóngxué dōu láile.
江 山：王英还没来，别的同学都来了。

Lǎoshī: Wáng Yīng zěnme la?
老 师：王英怎么啦？

Jiāng Shān: Bù zhīdao.
江 山：不知道。

Lǐqí: Tā zhù xuéshēng sùshè, měi tiān zài xuéxiào cāntīng chī zǎofàn.
里 奇：她住学生宿舍，每天在学校餐厅吃早饭。

Tiánzhōng: Wǒ xiǎng, xiànzài tā kěnéng zhèngzài chī zǎofàn.
田 中：我想，现在她可能正在吃早饭。

Jīn Róngnán: Dàgài hái zài shuìjiào ne.
金容南：大概还在睡觉呢。 [supposition]

Lǐqí: Bù kěnéng, tā kěndìng yǐjīng qǐchuáng le.
里 奇：不可能，她肯定已经起床了。

Mǎdīng: Nǐmen dōu cuò le. Wáng Yīng qù yīyuàn le.
马 丁：你们都错了。王英去医院了。 [information]

Lǎoshī: Zěnme, tā bìng le ma?
老 师：怎么，她病了吗？ [surprise]

Mǎdīng: Tā yǒudiǎnr bù shūfu.
马 丁：她有点儿不舒服。

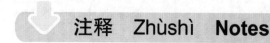

（一）每天在学校餐厅吃早饭 / 大概还在睡觉呢

The first 在 is a preposition which introduces a place expression; the second is an adverb, indicating an action in progress.

（二）她怎么啦

怎么，怎么样 and 怎么啦 are different. 怎么 is often used as an adverbial for asking about the manner; 怎么样 is often used as a predicate for inquiring about the situation. 怎么啦 indicates concern about the present situation, and has a tone of surprise.

E.g.　你们打算怎么去？　　我们打算坐飞机去。
　　　这些照片怎么样？　　这些照片很漂亮。
　　　他怎么啦？　　　　　他病了。

# 2.2

Jīntiān Zǎoshang Chīle Shénme?

今天 早上 吃了 什么?

What did you eat for breakfast this morning?

---

**Preliminary exercises**

1  Warm up

你吃早饭 / 午饭 / 晚饭了吧? 吃了什么?

2  Learn the following words and form correct sentences with the words under the teacher's guidance.

(1) 疼 我 肚子

(2) 请 客 我 今天, 请 吃 我 你 日餐

(3) 是 我 的 早餐 面包 牛奶 水果 和

(4) 医生 说, 得 吃 我 药, 得 打 针 还

(5) 着急 你 别, 有 我们 时间 还

(6) 干净 菜 这些 很, 新鲜 很 也

3  Listen to the recording and add 了 to the following sentences in the appropriate positions.

A: 昨天晚上你干什么＿＿＿＿＿?

B: 我去超市＿＿＿＿＿。

A: 买东西＿＿＿＿＿没有?

B: 买＿＿＿＿＿。

A: 买＿＿＿＿＿什么东西?

B: 买＿＿＿＿＿一些水果、几个面包。

Question:

In the above sentences, are 了 in different positions? Can you detect the rule concerning the positions of 了?

Listening script

③ A: 昨天晚上你干什么了?
B: 我去超市了。
A: 买东西了没有?
B: 买了。
A: 买了什么东西?
B: 买了一些水果、几个面包。

019 >>

**Words and expressions**

| | | | | |
|---|---|---|---|---|
| 1. | 新鲜 | ( Adj.) | xīnxiān | fresh |
| 2. | 干净 | ( Adj. ) | gānjìng | clean |
| 3. | 面包 | ( N. ) | miànbāo | bread |
| 4. | 片 | ( MW ) | piàn | *measure word for something flat and thin; slice*, piece |
| 5. | 牛奶 | ( N. ) | niúnǎi | milk |
| 6. | 杯 | ( MW ) | bēi | cup of …; glass of … |
| 7. | 生鱼片 | | shēngyúpiàn | slices of raw fish; sashimi |
| | 生 | ( Adj. ) | shēng | raw, uncooked |
| | 鱼片 | ( N. ) | yúpiàn | slices of fish |
| 8. | 昨天 | ( TW ) | zuótiān | yesterday |
| 9. | 请客 | ( V.O. ) | qǐngkè | treat; entertain guests |
| 10. | 吃药 | ( V.O.) | chīyào | take medicine |
| 11. | 着急 | ( Adj. ) | zháojí | worried, anxious |
| 12. | 说完 | | shuōwán | (be) finish(ed) saying |
| | 完 | ( V. ) | wán | finish(ed) |
| 13. | 医生 | ( N. ) | yīshēng | doctor |
| 14. | 肚子 | ( N. ) | dùzi | stomach |
| 15. | 疼 | ( Adj. ) | téng | aching |
| 16. | 厕所 | ( N. ) | cèsuǒ | washroom, toilet |
| 17. | 不过 | ( Conj. ) | búguò | but |

⚙ Listen to the dialogue and answer the following questions in Chinese.
（1）王英在哪儿?
（2）她哪儿不舒服?
（3）她昨天晚上吃了什么?
（4）她为什么很着急?

⚙ Listen to the recording while reading the text on the next page.

⚙ Read the text aloud and try not to look at the pinyin.

⚙ Work in groups and act out the conversation.

⚙ Activity
Skit: Seeing a doctor at a hospital.

## Vocabulary extension

| | | | | | | |
|---|---|---|---|---|---|---|
| 坏 | huài | bad; go bad; to spoil | 食品 | shípǐn | food |
| 卫生 | wèishēng | hygiene | 健康 | jiànkāng | health; healthy |
| 大夫 | dàifu | doctor, physician | 护士 | hùshi | nurse |
| 卫生间 | wèishēngjiān | bathroom, toilet | 洗手间 | xǐshǒujiān | washroom, toilet |
| 中医 | zhōngyī | doctor in traditional Chinese medicine | | | |
| 西医 | xīyī | doctor in Western medicine | | | |
| 中药 | zhōngyào | traditional Chinese medicine | | | |
| 西药 | xīyào | Western medicine | | | |

_____     _____

_____     _____

 **Text**

(Wang Ying is in the hospital.)

Wáng Yīng:　Yīshēng,　wǒ dùzi téng.
王　英：医生，我肚子疼。

Yīshēng:　Nǐ shì bu shì chīle　bù gānjìng de dōngxi?
医　生：你是不是吃了不干净的东西？

Wáng Yīng:　Méiyǒu a.
王　英：没有啊。

Yīshēng:　Jīntiān zǎoshang chīle　shénme?
医　生：今天早上吃了什么？

Wáng Yīng:　Chīle　jǐ piàn miànbāo,　hēle　yì bēi niúnǎi. …
王　英：吃了几片面包，喝了一杯牛奶。……

Búguò,　zuótiān wǎnshang péngyou qǐngkè,　wǒmen qùle xuéxiào
不过，昨天晚上　朋友 请客，我们去了学校

fùjìn de yí gè fàndiàn,　wǒ chīle hěn duō shēngyúpiàn.
附近的一个饭店，我吃了很多　生鱼片。 talking about past actions

Yīshēng:　Kěnéng shēngyúpiàn bú tài xīnxiān.　Nǐ děi chī yào,　hái děi…
医　生：可能 生鱼片不太新鲜。你得吃药，还得……

supposition　making a request

Wáng Yīng:　Duìbuqǐ…
王　英：对不起……

Yīshēng:　Bié zháojí,　wǒ hái méi shuōwán ne.　Nǐ děi chī yào,　hái děi…
医　生：别着急，我还没说完呢。你得吃药，还得……

Wáng Yīng:　Duìbuqǐ,　cèsuǒ zài nǎr?
王　英：对不起，厕所在哪儿？

注释　Zhùshì　**Notes**

（一）你是不是吃了不干净的东西

　　是不是 ... means "is it or is it not the case?" 是不是 is usually inserted between the subject and the predicate: S. 是不是 Pred.? E.g., 你是不是想买汽车?

　　是不是 can also be put at the beginning or the end of the sentence: 是不是 ... ?　/ ..., 是不是?　E.g., 是不是你想买汽车?　/你想买汽车 , 是不是?

（二）几片面包

　　A few slices of bread. Here, 几 is not a question word. It means "several, a few."

# 2.3 Language Points

❀ I. The Particle 了 (le) Indicating Completion of Action

In addition to indicating change, 了 is put after a verb to show completion of an action or the realization of an event.

　　E.g. （1）她已经来了。
　　　　（2）我昨天吃了很多生鱼片。


To express negation, add 没（有）before the verb and omit 了.
　　E.g. （1）她还没来。
　　　　（2）我昨天没吃生鱼片。


For the interrogative form, use: … 吗？ / … V. 没 V. … ？ / … 了没有？
　　E.g. （1）王英来了吗？
　　　　（2）王英来没来？
　　　　（3）王英来了没有？


If 了 follows a verb which has an object, a numeral or an attributive is usually placed before the object.
　　E.g. （1）我今天早上吃了几片面包，喝了一杯牛奶。
　　　　（2）我昨天吃了很多生鱼片。

❀ II. 在 (zài) and 正在 (zhèngzài) Indicating Ongoing Actions

In order to indicate an ongoing action, the adverb 在 or 正在 is used before the verb.
　　E.g. （1）你在干什么？
　　　　（2）我在看书。
　　　　（3）她可能还在睡觉呢。
　　　　（4）我们正在上课。

⚙ Use 在 or 正在 to complete the following sentences.
　　（1）现在，他＿＿＿＿＿＿＿＿＿＿＿＿＿＿＿。
　　（2）明天这个时候，他＿＿＿＿＿＿＿＿＿＿＿＿＿。
　　（3）老师进来的时候，我们＿＿＿＿＿＿＿＿＿＿＿＿＿。

⚙ Read the following sentences and decide whether the sentences require the usage of 了 or not. If needed, where should 了 be placed?

（1）他姓王，以前在北京工作。

（2）我们每天都要上汉语课。

（3）她已经起床，正在吃早饭。

（4）我们明天一起去打球。

（5）他没吃早饭，我也没吃。

（6）去年我们去北京旅游，我们拍很多照片。

 文化点　Wénhuàdiǎn　**Cultural notes**

Hospitals in China can be divided into comprehensive hospitals, specialized hospitals and clinics. Comprehensive hospitals usually have an E.R., outpatient facilities and inpatient facilities. There are two kinds of clinics: public ones (community health service centers) and private ones.

In China, the basic procedure of seeing a doctor is: pre-examination and registration; waiting to see the doctor; consultation with the doctor; paying fee and retrieving prescriptions, if any. In larger hospitals, there are many patients, so long queues are often expected.

In 1998, the Chinese government began to implement the Decision of the State Council on Establishing the Urban Employees' Basic Medical Insurance System and established a basic medical insurance system for urban employees nationwide. As of 2010, the new rural cooperative medical system covers most rural citizens.

*　　　*　　　*　　　*

Body:

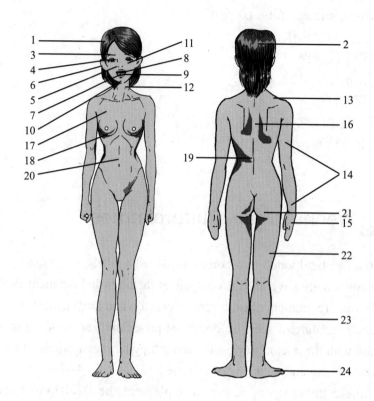

1. 头 tóu (head)　　　2. 头发 tóufa (hair)　　　3. 眉毛 méimao (eyebrow)

4. 眼睛 yǎnjing (eye)　　5. 鼻子 bízi (nose)　　　6. 耳朵 ěrduo (ear)

7. 嘴巴 zuǐba (mouth)　　8. 牙齿 yáchǐ (tooth)　　9. 舌头 shétou (tongue)

10. 下巴 xiàba (chin)　　11. 脸 liǎn (face)　　　12. 脖子 bózi (neck)

13. 肩膀 jiānbǎng (shoulder)　14. 手臂 shǒubì (arm)　　15. 手 shǒu (hand)

16. 背 bèi (back)　　　　17. 胸 xiōng (chest)　　18. 乳房 rǔfáng (breast)

19. 腰 yāo (waist)　　　20. 肚子 dùzi (abdomen)　21. 屁股 pìgu (buttock)

22. 大腿 dàtuǐ (thigh)　　23. 小腿 xiǎotuǐ (calf)　24. 脚 jiǎo (foot)

# Unit 3

## Tāmen Shì Shénme Shíhou Lái De?
## 他们 是 什么 时候 来 的?
## When Did They Arrive?

## Learning objectives

❀ Expressing times, location, manners, etc. of past actions

❀ Ways to connect topics

❀ Greetings

### Key sentences

Tāmen shì shénme shíhou lái de?

他们 是 什么 时候来 的?

When did they arrive?

Zhè běn shū shì shénme shíhou jiè de?

这 本 书 是 什么 时候借 的?

When did you borrow the book?

Nǐ zuótiān mǎi de nà zhāng xīn dìtú , néng bu néng jiè wǒ yòng yíxià?

你 昨天 买 的那 张 新地图, 能 不 能 借我 用一下?

Could you lend me the new map that you bought yesterday?

Chīle zǎofàn , wǒ yào péi wǒ bàmā qù Guójiā Bówùguǎn.

吃了 早饭, 我 要 陪我 爸妈 去 国家 博物馆。

After breakfast, I'm going to accompany my parents to the History

Museum.

# 3.1

Tāmen Shì Zuò Huǒchē Lái De

## 他们是坐火车来的

### They took the train here

## Preliminary exercises

1 Warm up

你今天是什么时候到学校的？是怎么来的？

2 Learn the following words and form correct sentences with the words under the teacher's guidance.

（1）来 我 这儿 第 一 次 是

（2）有用 地图 这 张 新 很

（3）感 兴趣 他 中国 经济 很 对

（4）借 你 的 词典 我 用 一下 可以 吗

（5）熟悉 中国 历史 文化 和 的 他 对 很，是"中国通" 一 位

（6）参观 我们 汽车 公司 去 一 个 今天 下午 先，

去 看 国家博物馆 一个 然后

3 Listen to the recording and fill in 了, 过 or 的 in the blanks.

（1）

A：你去_____上海吗？

B：去_____一次。

A：是什么时候去_____？

B：去年。

A：一个人去_____吗？

B：不是。跟我女朋友一起去_____。

（2）

A：你知道吗，他父母亲来看他_____。

B：是吗？！什么时候来_____？

A：昨天来_____。

B：是从北京来_____吗？

A：不是，是从香港来_____。

Question:

In the above sentences, 了 is used in some sentences while 过 or 的 is used in others. What are the reasons behind this?

## Words and expressions

| | | | | |
|---|---|---|---|---|
| 1. | 父母亲 | | fùmǔqīn | parents |
| | 父亲 | ( N. ) | fùqīn | father |
| | 母亲 | ( N. ) | mǔqīn | mother |
| 2. | 房间 | ( N. ) | fángjiān | room |
| 3. | 借 | ( V. ) | jiè | borrow, lend |
| 4. | 拿 | ( V. ) | ná | hold, take, bring |
| 5. | 参观 | ( V. ) | cānguān | visit; look around |
| 6. | 新 | ( Adj. ) | xīn | new |
| 7. | 先 | ( Adv. ) | xiān | first |
| 8. | 第 | | dì | prefix for ordinal numbers |
| 9. | 次 | ( MW ) | cì | measure word for frequency (number of times) |
| 10. | 政治 | ( N. ) | zhèngzhì | politics |
| 11. | 经济 | ( N. ) | jīngjì | economy |
| 12. | 历史 | ( N. ) | lìshǐ | history |
| 13. | 文化 | ( N. ) | wénhuà | culture |
| 14. | 国家 | ( N. ) | guójiā | country |
| 15. | 博物馆 | ( N. ) | bówùguǎn | museum |
| 16. | 对……感兴趣 / 有兴趣 | | duì … gǎnxìngqù / yǒuxìngqù | be interested in |
| | 兴趣 | ( N. ) | xìngqù | interest |
| 17. | 中国通 | | zhōngguótōng | an expert on China |

## Proper noun

| | | |
|---|---|---|
| 香港 | Xiānggǎng | Hong Kong |

⚙ Listen to the dialogue and answer the following questions in Chinese.
（1）马丁想跟高一飞借什么？
（2）马丁吃完早饭以后要干什么？
（3）马丁的父母亲是什么时候来的？从哪儿来的？怎么来的？
（4）马丁的父母亲对什么非常感兴趣？

⚙ Listen to the recording while reading the text on the next page.

⚙ Read the text aloud and try not to look at the pinyin.

⚙ Work in groups and act out the conversation.

⚙ Activity

Students and Teacher: (1) Where have you visited? When did you visit these places and how did you get there? What else can you tell us about your trip?
Or
(2) What fun or interesting things have you bought recently? Where did you buy these things and how much did you pay? What else can you tell us about what you bought?

## Vocabulary extension

| | | | | | | |
|---|---|---|---|---|---|---|
| 旅游 | lǚyóu | tour | | 景点 | jǐngdiǎn | scenic spot |
| 亲戚 | qīnqi | relative | | 同事 | tóngshì | colleague |
| 前年 | qiánnián | year before last | | 前天 | qiántiān | day before yesterday |
| 访问 | fǎngwèn | visit; call on | | | | |
| 拜访 | bàifǎng | (pol.) pay a visit; call on | | | | |
| 花 | huā | spend (time, money, etc.) | | | | |
| 汉学家 | hànxuéjiā | sinologist; expert of Sinology | | | | |

 **Text**

(On the campus of their Chinese college Martin and Gao Yifei meet at the dorm entrance one Saturday morning.)

Gāo Yīfēi:    Zǎofàn chī le ma?
高一飞：早饭吃了吗？ greeting

changing the subject

Mǎdīng:    Hái méiyǒu ne.    Ò,    duì le,    nǐ zuótiān mǎi de nà zhāng xīn  dìtú,
马　丁：还没有呢。哦，对了，你昨天买的那 张 新地图，

néng bu néng jiè wǒ yòng  yíxià?
能不能借我用一下？ making a request

Gāo Yīfēi:    Xíng a,    dào wǒ fángjiān qù ná ba.    Zěnme,    nǐ yào chūqù?
高一飞：行啊，到我房间去拿吧。怎么，你要出去？

Mǎdīng:    Chīle zǎofàn,    wǒ yào péi wǒ bàmā qù Guójiā Bówùguǎn.
马　丁：吃了早饭，我要陪我爸妈去国家博物馆。

Gāo Yīfēi:    Nǐ fùmǔqīn  lái le?
高一飞：你父母亲来了？

Mǎdīng:    Shì a.
马　丁：是啊。

Gāo Yīfēi:    Tāmen shì shénme shíhou lái de?
高一飞：他们是什么时候来的？ information

Mǎdīng:    Shàng ge  xīngqī.
马　丁：上个星期。

Gāo Yīfēi:    Shì cóng  Àodàlìyà    lái de ma?
高一飞：是从澳大利亚来的吗？

马　丁：Mǎdīng: Bú shì, tāmen xiān qùle Xiānggǎng, ránhòu qùle Běijīng, shàng ge

不是，他们先去了香港，然后去了北京，上个

xīngqī cóng Běijīng zuò huǒchē lái de.

星期从北京坐火车来的。

高一飞：Gāo Yīfēi: Tāmen yǐqián méi láiguo Zhōngguó ba?

他们以前没来过 中国 吧？ supposition

马　丁：Mǎdīng: Bù, láiguo, zhè yǐjīng shì dì-liù cì le. Tāmen duì Zhōngguó

不，来过，这已经是第六次了。他们对 中国

de jīngjì, lìshǐ, wénhuà fēicháng gǎn xìngqù.

的经济、历史、文化非常 感兴趣。

高一飞：Gāo Yīfēi: À, shì liǎng wèi "zhōngguótōng".

啊，是 两位 " 中国 通"。

## 注释　Zhùshì　Notes

（一）吃了早饭，我要陪我爸妈去国家博物馆

This means 吃了早饭以后，我要陪我爸妈去国家博物馆. V1 了 …（以后）V2 … indicates that the second action happens after the first action has finished.

（二）—— 他们以前没来过中国吧？

　　　　—— 不，来过。

不 is an answer to the person who is making a conjecture. It means "you are wrong in saying so." 来过 is a statement confirming a fact. Note that the way to answer a negative question in Chinese is different from English.

# 3.2

Zhè Běn Shū Shì Shénme Shíhou Jiè De?

## 这 本 书 是 什么 时候借 的?

## When did you borrow this book?

⬇ **Preliminary exercises**

💬 1 Warm up
你常常去图书馆借书吗? 一般借多长时间?

💬 2 Learn the following words and form correct sentences with the words under the teacher's guidance.
（1）做 生意 怎么 跟 中国人
（2）去 还 要 我 图书馆 一 本 书
（3）写 这 本 书 一 个 美国人 是 的
（4）过期 这 牛奶 了, 喝 不 能 了
（5）规定 是 这 公司 的, 知道 你 应该
（6）走 快 吧! 迟到 要 了 恐怕

💬 3 Fill in the blanks according to the recording.
（1）_____ 是谁写的?
（2）_____ 吃了没有?
（3）_____ 我听说过, 不过没看过。
（4）_____, 可以借我用一下吗?

Question:

How can the above sentences be translated into English? What are the differences between the Chinese and English ways of expression?

**Listening script**

3 （1）这本书是谁写的?
（2）早饭吃了没有?
（3）这本书我听说过, 不过没看过。
（4）你桌上的那张新地图, 可以借我用一下吗?

**Words and expressions**

| | | | | |
|---|---|---|---|---|
| 1. | 还 | ( V. ) | huán | return |
| 2. | 写 | ( V. ) | xiě | write |
| 3. | 下课 | ( V. O. ) | xiàkè | finish class; get out of class |
| 4. | 过期 | ( V. O. ) | guòqī | be overdue |
| 5. | 罚款 | ( V. O.) | fákuǎn | impose a fine |
| | 罚 | ( V. ) | fá | punish, penalize |
| | 款 | ( N. ) | kuǎn | a sum of money |
| 6. | 应该 | ( MV ) | yīnggāi | should; ought to |
| 7. | 图书馆 | ( N. ) | túshūguǎn | library |
| 8. | 生意 | ( N. ) | shēngyi | business |
| 9. | 规定 | ( N. & V. ) | guīdìng | rules; regulate, stipulate |
| 10. | 不错 | ( Adj. ) | búcuò | not bad; pretty good |
| 11. | 快 | ( Adj. & Adv.) | kuài | fast, quick(ly); hurry up; be about to |
| 12. | 厉害 | ( Adj. ) | lìhai | severe, fierce |
| 13. | 恐怕 | ( Adv. ) | kǒngpà | I'm afraid that ...; maybe, probably |
| 14. | 这么 | ( Adv. ) | zhème | like this; this way |
| 15. | 那么 | ( Adv. ) | nàme | like that; that way |
| 16. | 算了 | ( V. ) | suànle | let it go; forget it |

⚙ Listen to the dialogue and answer the following questions in Chinese.

（1）马丁从图书馆借了一本什么书？什么时候借的？

（2）马丁现在要去哪里？去干什么？

（3）王英想跟马丁借这本书，马丁为什么不借给她？

⚙ Listen to the recording while reading the text on the next page.

⚙ Read the text aloud and try not to look at the pinyin.

⚙ Work in groups and act out the conversation.

⚙ Activity

What interesting books have you read recently? Did you borrow them or buy them? Tell your classmates about the books and who wrote them.

## Vocabulary extension

| | | |
|---|---|---|
| 作者 | zuòzhě | writer, author |
| 参考 | cānkǎo | to consult; reference |
| 阅览室 | yuèlǎnshì | reading room |
| 办公室 | bàngōngshì | office |
| 教学楼 | jiàoxuélóu | classroom building |
| 学生证 | xuéshēngzhèng | student card |
| 借书证 | jièshūzhèng | library card  (literally: book-borrowing card) |

_____    _____

_____    _____

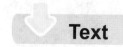

## Text

(Martin is walking to the library while Wang Ying is coming back from class; they meet on the way.)

Mǎdīng: Xiàkè la?
马 丁: 下课啦? greeting

Wáng Yīng: Xiàkè le. Nǐ qù nǎr?
王 英: 下课了。你去哪儿?

Mǎdīng: Qù túshūguǎn huán shū.
马 丁: 去图书馆还书。

Wáng Yīng: Shénme shū?
王 英: 什么书?

Mǎdīng: Yì běn Měiguórén xiě de shū, shūmíng jiào《 Zěnme gēn Zhōngguórén zuò
马 丁: 一本美国人写的书,书名叫《怎么跟 中国人做

shēngyi》. Nǐ kànguo ma?
生意》。你看过吗? information

Wáng Yīng: Tīngshuōguo, méi kànguo. Zhè běn shū zěnmeyàng?
王 英: 听说过,没看过。这本书怎么样?

Mǎdīng: Hěn búcuò. Nǐ yě yīnggāi kànkan.
马 丁: 很不错。你也应该看看。 suggestion

Wáng Yīng: Nà nǐ bié huán le, gěi wǒ kàn yíxià.
王 英: 那你别 还了,给我看一下。 making a request

Mǎdīng: Kǒngpà bù xíng. Jiù yào guòqī le.
马 丁: 恐怕不行。就要过期了。 refusal

Wáng Yīng: Zhè běn shū shì shénme shíhou jiè de?
王 英: 这本书是什么时候借的?

Mǎdīng: Shàng ge yuè èrshí hào. Kuài yí gè yuè le.
马 丁: 上 个月二十号。快一个月了。

Wáng Yīng: Guòle qī huì fákuǎn ba?
王　英：过了期会罚款吧？

Mǎdīng: Nà dāngrán. Túshūguǎn yǒu guīdìng, yàoshi guòqī bù huán, měi tiān
马　丁：那当然。图书馆有规定，要是过期不还，每天

fá yí kuài qián.
罚一块钱。

surprise　　　giving up　　　urging

Wáng Yīng: Wā, zhème lìhai! Nà suànle, nǐ kuài diǎnr qù huán ba.
王　英：哇，这么厉害！那算了，你快点儿去还吧。

## 注释　Zhùshì　Notes

（一）下课啦
啦 here is a fusion of the words 了 and 啊.

（二）快一个月了
This means "nearly one month."

（三）过了期会罚款吧？
Here 会 indicates the possibility. Another example: 这么晚了，我想他不会来了。

# 3.3 Language Points

## ❧ I. 是……的 (shì…de)

The structure 是 … 的 is used when both parties know that an action has taken place, but the speaker needs to point out when, where and how it took place. 是 can be omitted in this pattern.

> **（是）+ when / where / how … + V. + 的**

A：你看，这件衬衫怎么样?
B：不错。你（是）什么时候买的?
A：我（是）昨天买的。
B：你（是）在哪儿买的?
A：我（是）在我家旁边的一个小商店买的。
B：（是）多少钱买的?
A：九十块。

If the verb is followed by an object, the object normally follows 的，but sometimes precedes 的.
今天我（是）早上六点起的床。
今天我（是）早上六点起床的。

## ❧ II. Verb Phrases and Clauses Used As Attributives

Verbs, verb phrases, and clauses can be used as attributives, just like nouns, adjectives, and numerals. But, when used for this purpose, they must be followed by 的.
（1）你去过的地方真多啊!
（2）这是我昨天买的衬衫。
（3）我工作的地方离这儿很远。
（4）这些都是我在中国拍的照片。
（5）这是喝茶的杯子，那是喝咖啡的杯子。

## ❧ III. Topicalization

Chinese is a topic-prominent language. Normally, the preceding part of a sentence is a specific element functioning as the topic, while the subsequent part is the declaration, or the comment on it. In the following examples, the underlined parts are the topics:

（1）我肚子疼。
（2）她瘦瘦的，高高的，头发长长的。
（3）你昨天买的那张新地图，能不能借我用一下？

In a conversation, the second speaker may continue to talk about certain thing or events introduced by the first speaker. To smooth the conversation, the thing introduced will be placed at the beginning of the sentence. For example:

A：我想去买一张中国地图。
B：中国地图我有，你要看吗？

Other examples：
A：我从图书馆借了两本书，一本是《说什么》，一本是《怎么说》。
B：《说什么》我看过，很不错；《怎么说》我没看过，你能给我看看吗？

Sometimes the receiver of an action appears at the beginning of the sentence as the topic, while the doer does not appear. Thus, the voice seems to be passive. But in this kind of Chinese sentence, there is usually no special indication of subject/doer, unless its omission causes some misunderstanding. In fact, this kind of sentences also indicates the relation of the topic to its comment.

（1）早饭吃了吗？
（2）这本书是什么时候借的？

⚙ Complete the following sentences.
（1）这些都是_____照片。（在长城上　拍）
（2）这是_____新地图。（我　昨天　买）
（3）_____地方很远。（我　工作）
（4）_____地方真多啊！（你　去）
（5）这本书_____。（很多人　喜欢）
（6）这本书_____？（你可以　借给我）
（7）这本书_____。（上个月　借）

## 文化点　Wénhuàdiǎn　Cultural notes

"Nǐ hǎo!" is not a traditional Chinese greeting. It is now used mostly by the more educated people in cities. It would be rather monotonous if you always said "nǐ hǎo!" when greeting people. In actuality, the Chinese have many different ways of greeting people. The general principle is to use expressions that show concern for the people one encounters, according to the time of day and the specific situation. Sometimes the expression may be a greeting, but sometimes it seems more like a statement of obvious fact.

For example, suppose it is lunchtime and you run into a friend at the entrance to the library. You can say, "Chīle ma?" (Have you eaten?) If you are walking into the dining hall just as your friend, who just finished eating, is leaving, you could say, "Chīwán le?" (Finished eating?)

When you notice that your friend is just about to go out, you might say, "Qù nǎr a?" (Where are you going?) If your friend is a student, it should be obvious that he is going to class, so you might simply say, "Qù shàngkè ya?" (Going to class?) When you come across a friend who is just coming out of a classroom, you might say, "Xiàkè le?" (Finished your class?)

It may seem that questions like, "Finished eating?" or "Finished class?" are rather unnecessary, but they are actually greetings.

Answers to these questions can be quite varied, too.

For example:

— Nǐ qù nǎr? (Where are you going?)

— Chūqù yíxià. (Just going out.)

Or just give a smile, a nod, or a vague gesture. You may, of course, give a detailed answer as to where you are going. It all depends on your relationship with the other person, the significance of where you are going or whether you have time to stop to chat.

Another way of greeting someone is simply to directly address the person by name or title; this is also considered a form of greeting.

For example:

— Hèi, Xiǎo Zhāng. (Hey, Xiao Zhang.)

— Ài, Wáng lǎoshī. (Hi, Professor Wang.)

# Unit 4

## Jīntiān Nǐ Chuān De Zhēn Piàoliang
## 今天 你 穿 得 真 漂亮
### You're Dressed So Beautifully Today

## Learning objectives

* Comments on actions and states
* Expressing compliments and wishes
* Wishing someone a Happy Birthday
* The zodiac animals

## Key sentences

Jīntiān nǐ chuān de zhēn piàoliang.
今天 你 穿 得 真 漂亮。
You're dressed so beautifully today.

Tā jiù shì nàge chànggē chàng de fēicháng hǎotīng de nǚháizi.
她 就 是 那个 唱歌 唱 得 非常 好听 的 女孩子。
She is the girl whose singing is so pleasant to hear.

Zhù nǐ yuèláiyuè piàoliang , yuèláiyuè niánqīng.
祝 你 越来越 漂亮, 越来越 年轻。
May you become prettier and prettier, and younger and younger.

Wǒ ya , jiǔ hē de yuè duō , Hànyǔ jiù shuō de yuè liúlì.
我 呀, 酒 喝 得 越 多, 汉语 就 说 得 越 流利。
The more I drink, the more fluently I speak Chinese.

# 4.1

Tā Chànggē Chàng De Fēicháng Hǎotīng

## 她 唱歌 唱 得 非常 好听

## She sings very well

**Preliminary exercises**

① Warm up

你会唱歌吗？唱得怎么样？

你会跳舞吗？跳得怎么样？

② Learn the following words and form correct sentences with the words under the teacher's guidance.

（1）会 唱 他 歌 中国

（2）跳 舞 一 个 请 你 可以 吗

（3）好听 他 唱 歌 得 特别

（4）优美 她 跳 舞 得 非常

（5）有 外事 活动 我 一 个 今天

（6）见 中国 国家 主席 美国 总统 我 都 和 过

③ Listen to the recording and complete the following sentences.

（1）你来_____。

（2）你回答_____。

（3）今天她穿_____。

（4）他唱歌_____。

（5）她跳舞_____。

Question:

Summarize the syntax of the five sentences above.

**Words and expressions**

| | | | | |
|---|---|---|---|---|
| 1. | 唱歌 | ( V. O. ) | chànggē | sing |
| | 唱 | ( V. ) | chàng | sing |
| | 歌 | ( N. ) | gē | song |
| 2. | 跳舞 | ( V. O. ) | tiàowǔ | dance |
| | 跳 | ( V. ) | tiào | jump |
| | 舞 | ( N. ) | wǔ | dance |
| 3. | 好听 | ( Adj. ) | hǎotīng | pleasant to hear |
| 4. | 好看 | ( Adj. ) | hǎokàn | beautiful, good-looking |
| 5. | 优美 | ( Adj. ) | yōuměi | graceful, fine |
| 6. | 晚 | ( Adj. ) | wǎn | late |
| 7. | 早 | ( Adj. ) | zǎo | early |
| 8. | 特别 | ( Adv. & Adj. ) | tèbié | especially; special |
| 9. | 主席 | ( N. ) | zhǔxí | chairman |
| 10. | 总统 | ( N. ) | zǒngtǒng | president |
| 11. | 外事 | ( N. ) | wàishì | foreign affairs |
| 12. | 活动 | ( N. & V. ) | huódòng | activity; exercise |
| 13. | 问题 | ( N. ) | wèntí | question, problem |
| 14. | 回答 | ( V. ) | huídá | answer, reply |
| 15. | 见 | ( V. ) | jiàn | see, meet |
| 16. | 去年 | ( TW ) | qùnián | last year |
| 17. | 得 | ( Part. ) | de | used to introduce a complement to show degree |

Unit 4

⚙ Listen to the dialogue and answer the following questions in Chinese.
（1）里奇今天有什么活动？
（2）里奇的女朋友怎么样？
（3）里奇和他的女朋友是什么时候认识的？
（4）马丁为什么说自己"太晚了"？

⚙ Listen to the recording while reading the text on the next page.

⚙ Read the text aloud and try not to look at the pinyin.

⚙ Work in groups and act out the conversation.

⚙ Activity

Students: What talents or skills do you have? How developed is your talent or skill? For example:
你会说法语吗？说得怎么样？
你会打篮球吗？打得怎么样？
你会做中国菜吗？做得怎么样？
......

## Vocabulary extension

| | | | | | | |
|---|---|---|---|---|---|---|
| 好吃 | hǎochī | tasty | 流利 | liúlì | fluent(ly) |
| 专业 | zhuānyè | specialty; professional | 马马虎虎 | mǎmǎhūhū | so-so, passable |
| 认真 | rènzhēn | conscientious, serious | 帅 | shuài | handsome |
| 女王 | nǚwáng | queen | 总督 | zǒngdū | governor-general |
| 总理 | zǒnglǐ | premier | 首相 | shǒuxiàng | prime minister |
| 省长 | shěngzhǎng | governor of a province | 领导 | lǐngdǎo | leader |
| 校长 | xiàozhǎng | principal (of a school), president (of a college or university) | | | |

_____          _____

_____          _____

(Martin encounters his classmate, Richie, on the street.)

Mǎdīng:　Jīntiān　nǐ chuān de zhēn piàoliang　a.

马　丁：今天你 穿 得 真 漂亮 啊。

compliment

Lǐqí:　Wǒ jīntiān yǒu "wàishì"　huódòng.

里　奇：我今天有 "外事" 活动。

Mǎdīng:　Wàishì huódòng?　Qù jiàn Zhōngguó guójiā　zhǔxí,　háishi

马　丁：外事活动？去见 中国 国家主席，还是

Měiguó zǒngtǒng?

美国 总统？

Lǐqí:　Dōu bú shì.　Qù jiàn wǒ nǚpéngyou de　fùmǔqīn.　Zhè shì wǒ　dì-yī cì

里　奇：都不是。去见 我女朋友的父母亲。这是我第一次

qù tā jiā.

去她家。

Mǎdīng:　Nǐ nǚpéngyou shì shéi ya?

马　丁：你女朋友是 谁呀？

curiosity

Lǐqí:　Nǐ bù zhīdao?　Jiù shì Xiǎo Zhāng a.

里　奇：你不知道？就是 小 张 啊。

Mǎdīng:　Xiǎo Zhāng? Jiù shì nàge tèbié　kě'ài,　tèbié piàoliang de　nǚháizi?

马　丁：小 张？就是 那个特别可爱、特别漂亮的女孩子？

Lǐqí:　Shì a.

里　奇：是啊。

马　丁：那个唱歌唱得非常好听的女孩子？
Mǎdīng: Nàge chànggē chàng de fēicháng hǎotīng de nǚháizi?

里　奇：是啊。
Lǐqí: Shì a.

马　丁：那个跳舞跳得特别优美的女孩子？
Mǎdīng: Nàge tiàowǔ tiào de tèbié yōuměi de nǚháizi?

里　奇：是啊。
Lǐqí: Shì a.

马　丁：她是你女朋友？
Mǎdīng: Tā shì nǐ nǚpéngyou?

里　奇：是啊。
Lǐqí: Shì a.

马　丁：你们什么时候认识的？
Mǎdīng: Nǐmen shénme shíhou rènshi de?

里　奇：去年。——你还有什么问题？
Lǐqí: Qùnián. — Nǐ hái yǒu shénme wèntí?

马　丁：没有了。(to himself) 嗨，我……太晚了！
Mǎdīng: Méiyǒu le. Hài, wǒ … tài wǎn le!

里　奇：太晚了？你什么意思？
Lǐqí: Tài wǎn le? Nǐ shénme yìsi?

# 4.2

Jīntiān Mǎdīng De Hànyǔ shuō De Tèbié Liúlì
## 今天 马丁 的 汉语 说 得 特别 流利
### Martin is speaking Chinese especially fluently today

⬇ **Preliminary exercises**

1️⃣ Warm up

你知道自己的生肖吗?

祝贺别人生日的时候,你对他说什么?

2️⃣ Learn the following words and form correct sentences with the words under the teacher's guidance.

(1) 祝 快乐 生日 你

(2) 流利 汉语 他 说 很 得

(3) 吃 生日 蛋糕 我们 一起 吧

(4) 年轻 我们 老师 的 很 还

(5) 喝 酒 很多 我们 昨天 晚上 了

(6) 是 生日礼物 送给 你 这 条 玉龙 我 的

3️⃣ Listen to the recording and complete the following sentences.

(1) 东西_____贵了。

(2) 他跑得_____快了。

(3) 他的汉语_____说_____流利了。

(4) 你们吃得_____多,我就_____高兴。

Question:

What are the meanings of the above sentences? Summarize the usages of 越来越 … and 越 … 越 ….

## Words and expressions

| | | | | |
|---|---|---|---|---|
| 1. | 生日 | ( N. ) | shēngrì | birthday |
| 2. | 生肖 | ( N. ) | shēngxiào | the 12 animals of the zodiac used to denote the year of a person's birth |
| 3. | 属 | ( V. ) | shǔ | be born in the year of |
| 4. | 祝 | ( V. ) | zhù | wish (expressing good wishes) |
| 5. | 快乐 | ( Adj. ) | kuàilè | merry, happy |
| 6. | 送 | ( V. ) | sòng | give (something as a gift) |
| 7. | 礼物 | ( N. ) | lǐwù | gift |
| 8. | 玉 | ( N. ) | yù | jade |
| 9. | 年轻 | ( Adj. ) | niánqīng | young |
| 10. | 流利 | ( Adj. ) | liúlì | fluent |
| 11. | 明白 | ( V. & Adj. ) | míngbai | understand; clear |
| 12. | 字 | ( N. ) | zì | character |
| 13. | 蛋糕 | ( N. ) | dàngāo | cake |
| 14. | 酒 | ( N. ) | jiǔ | wine, liquor |
| 15. | 干杯 | ( V. O. ) | gānbēi | drink a toast; "Cheers!" |
| 16. | 咱们 | ( Pron. ) | zánmen | we |
| 17. | 越来越…… | | yuèláiyuè … | more and more |
| 18. | 越……越…… | | yuè … yuè … | the more … the more … |

⚙ Listen to the dialogue and answer the following questions in Chinese.

（1）今天是谁的生日？

（2）小张属什么的？今年多大？

（3）马丁送给小张一件什么礼物？他祝小张什么？

⚙ Listen to the recording while reading the text on the next page.

⚙ Read the text aloud and try not to look at the pinyin.

⚙ Work in groups and act out the conversation.

⚙ Activity

Find out which classmate will next celebrate his or her birthday. Each student should then give him or her a birthday wish in Chinese.

## Vocabulary extension

| 过 | guò | go through; to pass | 庆祝 | qìngzhù | to celebrate |
| 点 | diǎn | to light | 蜡烛 | làzhú | candle |
| 祝贺 | zhùhè | congratulation | 祝愿 | zhùyuàn | to wish; wish |
| 葡萄酒 | pútaojiǔ | wine | 啤酒 | píjiǔ | beer |
| 工作顺利 | gōngzuò-shùnlì | work smoothly | | | |
| 学习进步 | xuéxí-jìnbù | make progress in study | | | |

## Text

(At Xiao Zhang's birthday party.)

Gāo Yīfēi: Zhù nǐ shēngrì kuàilè!

高一飞：祝你生日快乐！　　　good wishes

Xiǎo Zhāng: Xièxie!

小　张：谢谢！

Mǎdīng: Zhè shì wǒ sòng gěi nǐ de yí jiàn xiǎo lǐwù. Nǐ shǔ lóng,

马　丁：这是我 送给你的一件小礼物。你 属龙，

sòng nǐ yì tiáo yùlóng.

送 你一条玉龙。　　　suggestion

Xiǎo Zhāng: Āiyā, nǐ tài kèqi le, xièxie! Lái, zánmen chī dàngāo ba.

小　张：哎呀，你太客气了，谢谢！来，咱们吃蛋糕吧。

Mǎdīng: Nǐ kàn, dàngāo shang xiě de shì shénme?

马　丁：(to Gao Yifei) 你看，蛋糕上写的是什么？

Gāo Yīfēi: Zhè bú shì "shēngrì kuàilè" sì gè zì ma?

高一飞：这不是"生日快乐"四个字吗？　　　good wishes

Mǎdīng: Ò, "shēngrì kuàilè" … Xiǎo Zhāng, zhù nǐ yuèláiyuè piàoliang,

马　丁：哦，"生日快乐"……小　张，祝你越来越漂亮，

yuèláiyuè niánqīng. Jīnnián èrshí, míngnián shíbā.

越来越年轻，今年二十，明年十八。

Lǐqí: Jīntiān Mǎdīng de Hànyǔ shuō de tèbié liúlì.

里　奇：今天马丁的汉语说得特别流利。

马　丁：<br>
Mǎdīng: Wǒ ya, jiǔ hē de yuè duō, Hànyǔ jiù shuō de yuè liúlì.<br>
马　丁：我呀，酒喝得越多，汉语就说得越流利。

Xiǎo Zhǎng: À, wǒ míngbai le, nǐ de yìsi shì —<br>
小　张：啊，我明白了，你的意思是——

Lǐqí: Tā hái xiǎng zài hē yì bēi.<br>
里　奇：他还想再喝一杯。

Mǎdīng: Hǎo ba. Lái, gānbēi!<br>
马　丁：好吧。来，干杯！

## 注释　Zhùshì　Notes

（一）咱们吃蛋糕吧

"咱们" = 我（们）+ 你（们）

（二）这不是"生日快乐"四个字吗

Aren't those the four characters for "Happy Birthday?"

不是 … 吗 is a rhetorical question, implying "it surely is …."

（三）今年二十，明年十八

This year you're twenty, but next year you'll be eighteen.

This alludes to a well-known advertisement which says "You are getting younger and younger, more and more beautiful."

（四）酒喝得越多，汉语就说得越流利

The more I drink, the more fluently I speak Chinese.

越 … 越 … means, "the more …, the more …." 越 is an adverb which must be placed in front of a verb or an adjective. It cannot precede the subject.

# 4.3 Language Points

❖ I. V. / Adj. + 得 + Predicative Complement

To further describe an action or a state, a verb or an adjective may take a verb or an adjective phrase as its complement. The complement provides information concerning the manner, result, degree, or evaluation of the action or the state. 得 is used as a connector between the verb/adjective and its complement.

## V. / Adj. + 得 + Predicative Complement

（1）他忙得没空吃饭。
（2）昨天他来得很晚。
（3）今天你穿得特别漂亮。
（4）这本书写得非常有意思。

If the verb has an object, the object cannot simply follow the verb, but must be placed before the complement, using one of the following patterns:

**(1) V. O. + V. 得 + Predicative Complement**
（1）她唱歌唱得很好听。
（2）她跳舞跳得很优美。
（3）他说汉语说得很流利。

**(2) O. + V. 得 + Predicative Complement**
（1）她歌唱得很好听。
（2）她舞跳得很优美。
（3）他汉语说得很流利。

❖ II. Verb-Object Compounds

Some disyllabic or polysyllabic expressions are regarded as single verbs with all the syllables normally linked together, but sometimes, other elements may be inserted between the syllables. Strictly speaking, many of these compounds are not verbs but rather verb-object compounds. The following are all V-O compounds:

见面　请客　睡觉　唱歌　跳舞　上课　吃饭　喝酒……

For example, it seems that 见面 is a single verb, but 见 and 面 can actually be separated. 见 is the verb, while 面 is the object, thus, 见面 itself cannot affect an object. We can say any of the following:

（1）我昨天跟他见面了。

（2）我昨天跟他见了面。

（3）我想跟你见一个面。

As for 跳舞, we can say:

（1）她跳了一个舞。

（2）她跳舞跳得很优美。

（3）她舞跳得很优美。

Or simply:

（4）她跳得很优美。

⚙ Choose the correct sentence in each group.

（1）A. 我明天要见面一位朋友。
　　B. 我明天要见一位朋友。
　　C. 我明天要跟一位朋友见。

（2）A. 我在他家吃过饭。
　　B. 我在他家吃饭过。
　　C. 我吃饭过他家。

（3）A. 他唱歌得很好听。
　　B. 他唱歌唱得很好听。
　　C. 他的唱歌很好听。

（4）A. 他写汉字得很漂亮。
　　B. 他汉字写得很漂亮。
　　C. 他的写汉字很漂亮。

（5）A. 他每天起床得很早。
　　B. 他每天起得很早。
　　C. 他每天很早得起床。

文化点　Wénhuàdiǎn　**Cultural notes**

In Chinese traditional culture, there are 12 animals used to mark a cycle of 12 years; these 12 animals form the Chinese zodiac (shí'èr shēngxiào). The sequence of zodiac animals is: rat (shǔ), ox (niú), tiger (hǔ), rabbit (tù), dragon (lóng), snake (shé), horse (mǎ), sheep (yáng), monkey (hóu), rooster (jǐ), dog (gǒu), and pig (zhū). When a person is born in a certain year according to the lunar calendar, he or she "belongs to" (shǔ) that animal. For instance, people born in the lunar year of 1976, 1988, 2000, and 2012 are dragons; those born in the lunar year of 1977, 1989, 2001, and 2013 are snakes.

Unit 4

**The 12 animals:**

鼠 (shǔ) rat      牛 (niú) ox      虎 (hǔ) tiger

兔 (tù) rabbit      龙 (lóng) dragon      蛇 (shé) snake

马 (mǎ) horse      羊 (yáng) sheep      猴 (hóu) monkey

鸡 (jī) rooster      狗 (gǒu) dog      猪 (zhū) pig

# Unit 5

## Wǒ Jiāxiāng De Tiānqì Bǐ Zhèr Hǎo
## 我 家乡 的 天气 比 这儿 好
## The Weather in My Hometown Is Better Than Here

## Learning objectives

* Expressing comparisons
* Talking about the weather
* Talking about seasons and the climate

### Key sentences

Wǒ jiāxiāng méiyǒu zhème rè.
我 家乡 没有 这么 热。
It's not so hot in my hometown.

Wǒ jiāxiāng de xiàtiān bǐ zhèr liángkuai duō le.
我 家乡 的 夏天 比 这儿 凉快 多了。
Summer in my hometown is much cooler than here.

Nǐ jiāxiāng de tiānqì gēn zhèr yíyàng ma?
你 家乡 的 天气 跟 这儿 一样 吗?
Is the weather in your hometown the same as here?

Nà shíhou hěn shǎo xià yǔ, yě bù guā fēng, tiānqì hǎojí le.
那 时候 很 少 下雨, 也 不 刮 风, 天气 好极了。
It doesn't rain much and it's not windy; the weather is very nice during that time.

## 5.1

# 我 家乡 没有 这么 热

## It's not so hot in my hometown

⬇

### Preliminary exercises

① **Warm up**

这里一年有几个季节？你喜欢哪个季节，为什么？

② Learn the following words and form correct sentences with the words under the teacher's guidance.

（1）听 天气 预报 我 每天 都

（2）有 四个 季节 一年 冬 春 秋 夏

（3）在 南方 中国 的，没有 暖气 冬天

（4）没有 冬天 我 家乡，有 夏天 只

（5）热 外面 房间 很，凉快 里面 房间 非常

（6）冷 外面 房间 很，暖和 里面 房间 非常

③ Listen to the recording and then write down the four people's replies. Listen to the recording again to check your answers.

你家乡的夏天有这么热吗？

（1）_____。

（2）_____。

（3）_____。

（4）_____。

Question:

What are the meanings of the four sentences?

③（1）我家乡的夏天比这儿更热。
（2）我家乡的夏天没有这么热。
（3）我家乡的夏天比这儿热多了。
（4）我家乡的夏天跟这儿差不多一样儿。

🔊 Listening script

**Words and expressions**

| 1. | 季节 | ( N. ) | jìjié | season |
|----|------|--------|-------|--------|
| 2. | 春天 | ( TW ) | chūntiān | spring |
| 3. | 夏天 | ( TW ) | xiàtiān | summer |
| 4. | 秋天 | ( TW ) | qiūtiān | autumn, fall |
| 5. | 冬天 | ( TW ) | dōngtiān | winter |
| 6. | 热 | ( Adj. ) | rè | hot |
| 7. | 暖和 | ( Adj. ) | nuǎnhuo | warm |
| 8. | 凉快 | ( Adj. ) | liángkuai | cool |
| 9. | 冷 | ( Adj. ) | lěng | cold |
| 10. | 听 | ( V. ) | tīng | listen |
| 11. | 天气 | ( N. ) | tiānqì | weather |
| 12. | 预报 | ( V. ) | yùbào | forecast |
| 13. | 温度 | ( N. ) | wēndù | temperature |
| 14. | 低 | ( Adj. ) | dī | low |
| 15. | 度 | ( MW ) | dù | degree (a measure word for temperature, etc.) |
| 16. | 左右 | ( Part. ) | zuǒyòu | about, around; … or so |
| 17. | 暖气 | ( N. ) | nuǎnqì | (central) heating |
| 18. | 家乡 | ( N. ) | jiāxiāng | hometown |
| 19. | 比 | ( Prep. ) | bǐ | than |
| 20. | 更 | ( Adv. ) | gèng | more |

Unit
5

⚙ Listen to the dialogue and answer the following questions in Chinese.
  （1）今天的最高温度是多少？
  （2）在高一飞的家乡，现在天气怎么样？
  （3）在里奇的家乡，现在天气怎么样？

⚙ Listen to the recording while reading the text on the next page.

⚙ Read the text aloud and try not to look at the pinyin.

⚙ Work in groups and act out the conversation.

⚙ Activity
Students: Talk about the seasons in your hometown.

## Vocabulary extension

| 摄氏 | shèshì | Celsius, centigrade | 华氏 | huáshì | Fahrenheit |
|---|---|---|---|---|---|
| 气温 | qìwēn | air temperature | 气候 | qìhòu | climate |
| 平均 | píngjūn | average | 一般 | yìbān | generally |
| 空调 | kōngtiáo | air-conditioner | 电扇 | diànshàn | electric fan |
| 雨季 | yǔjì | rainy season | 旱季 | hànjì | dry season |
| 全年 | quánnián | the whole year | | | |

_____     _____

_____     _____

# Text

(Richie and Gao Yifei are talking about the weather in their hometowns.)

Lǐqí: Zhēn rè ya!
里　奇：真热呀！

Gāo Yīfēi: Rè?
高一飞：热？

Lǐqí: Nǐ bú rè?
里　奇：你不热？

Gāo Yīfēi: Hái kěyǐ.
高一飞：还可以。

Lǐqí: Jīntiān de tiānqì yùbào nǐ tīngle méiyǒu?
里　奇：今天的天气预报你听了没有？

Gāo Yīfēi: Tīng le. Zuì gāo wēndù sānshíyī dù, hái bú shì zuì rè de shíhou.
高一飞：听了。最高温度三十一度，还不是最热的时候。

Lǐqí: Xiànzài nǐ jiāxiāng de tiānqì zěnmeyàng? Yǒu zhème rè ma?
里　奇：现在你家乡的天气怎么样？有这么热吗？ ⌐comparison⌐

Gāo Yīfēi: Bǐ zhèr gèng rè. Nǐ jiāxiāng ne?
高一飞：比这儿更热。你家乡呢？ comparison

Lǐqí: Méiyǒu zhème rè. Wǒ jiāxiāng de xiàtiān bǐ zhèr liángkuai duō le.
里　奇：没有这么热。我家乡的夏天比这儿凉快多了。 comparison

Gāo Yīfēi: Nà dōngtiān ne?
高一飞：那冬天呢？

Lǐqí: Bǐ zhèr lěng yìdiǎnr. Zuì dī wēndù líng xià bā dù zuǒyòu.
里 奇：比这儿冷一点儿，最低温度零下八度左右。

comparison

Gāo Yīfēi: Nàme lěng a.
高一飞：那么冷啊。

Lǐqí: Búguò, fángjiān li dōu yǒu nuǎnqì, fēicháng nuǎnhuo, yìdiǎnr
里 奇：不过，房间里都有暖气，非常 暖和，一点儿

yě bù lěng.
也不冷。

## 注释 Zhùshì Notes

（一）还可以

还可以 indicates that the situation is not so bad; it is still tolerable.

（二）最高温度三十一度

This means "31 degrees Celsius." In China, the Celsius (shèshì) system of indicating temperature is used, rather than the Fahrenheit (huáshì) system.

（三）一点儿也不冷

一点儿, (not) at all / (not) a bit, is used for emphasis in a negative sentence. Other examples: 一点儿也不漂亮 / 一点儿也不知道 / 一点儿也没吃.

# 5.2

## 你 家乡 的 天气 跟 这儿 一样 吗?

### Is the weather in your hometown the same as here?

**Unit 5**

---

### ↓ Preliminary exercises

**1** Warm up

今天的天气预报你听了吗？请向同学们介绍一下明天的天气。

**2** Learn the following words and form correct sentences with the words under the teacher's guidance.

（1）是 春天 季节 美丽 最 的

（2）舒服 秋天 那里 的 极了 真是

（3）晴 多云 到 上午 明天，有 雨 下午 有时

（4）下 雪 冬天 很 少 这里 的，刮 风 不 也

（5）长 夏天 现在 越来越 了，短 春天 越来越 了

（6）去 游泳 夏天 我们 常常，去 滑雪 冬天 我们 常常

**3** Listen to the recording and then write down the four people's replies. Listen to the recording again to check your answers.

你家乡的春天跟这儿差不多吧？

（1）_____。

（2）_____。

（3）_____。

（4）_____。

Question:

What are the meanings of the four sentences above?

**Listening script**

**3**（1）我家乡的春天跟这儿一样美。

（2）我家乡的春天没有这儿暖和。

（3）我家乡的春天比这儿暖和多了。

（4）我家乡的春天比这儿来得早一点儿。

## Words and expressions

| | | | | |
|---|---|---|---|---|
| 1. | 晴天 | ( N. ) | qíngtiān | sunny day |
| 2. | 多云 | ( Adj. ) | duōyún | cloudy |
| 3. | 下雨 | ( V.O. ) | xiàyǔ | rain |
| | 雨 | ( N. ) | yǔ | rain |
| 4. | 下雪 | ( V.O. ) | xiàxuě | snow |
| | 雪 | ( N. ) | xuě | snow |
| 5. | 刮风 | ( V.O. ) | guāfēng | wind (is) blowing; (to be) windy |
| | 刮 | ( V. ) | guā | blow |
| | 风 | ( N. ) | fēng | wind |
| 6. | 滑雪 | ( V. O. ) | huáxuě | ski |
| | 滑 | ( V. & Adj. ) | huá | ski, slip; slippery |
| 7. | 滑冰 | ( V. O. ) | huábīng | skate |
| | 冰 | ( N. ) | bīng | ice |
| 8. | 游泳 | ( V. O. ) | yóuyǒng | swim |
| | 游 | ( V. ) | yóu | swim |
| 9. | 美 | ( Adj. ) | měi | beautiful |
| 10. | 短 | ( Adj. ) | duǎn | short |
| 11. | 一样 | ( Adj. ) | yíyàng | the same |
| 12. | 差不多 | ( Adj.) | chàbuduō | about the same |
| 13. | ……极了 | | …jí le | very, extremely |
| 14. | 枫叶 | ( N. ) | fēngyè | maple leaf |
| 15. | 常常 | ( Adv. ) | chángcháng | often |
| 16. | 有的时候（有时候／有时） | | yǒude shíhou (yǒu shíhou / yǒushí ) | sometimes |
| 17. | 很少 | | hěn shǎo | seldom |

⚙ Listen to the dialogue and answer the following questions in Chinese.
（1）高一飞家乡的天气怎么样？
（2）王英家乡的天气怎么样？
（3）高一飞最喜欢什么季节？为什么？王英呢？

⚙ Listen to the recording while reading the text on the next page.

⚙ Read the text aloud and try not to look at the pinyin.

⚙ Work in groups and act out the conversation.

⚙ Activity

Students: Do you know about the different climates in China? Compare the four seasons in China's North and South. Then compare the four seasons of your hometown to that of China.

## Vocabulary extension

| 冰天雪地 | bīngtiān-xuědì | world of ice and snow | | | |
| 四季如春 | sìjì-rúchūn | (it's) like spring all year | | | |
| 四季分明 | sìjì-fēnmíng | the four seasons are quite distinctive | | | |
| 北方 | běifāng | northern area | 南方 | nánfāng | southern area |
| 潮湿 | cháoshī | humid | 干燥 | gānzào | dry |
| 阴天 | yīntiān | overcast, cloudy | 太阳 | tàiyáng | sun |
| 月亮 | yuèliang | moon | 星星 | xīngxing | star |
| 空气 | kōngqì | air | 天空 | tiānkōng | sky |

_____          _____

_____          _____

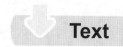

**Text**

(Wang Ying and Gao Yifei are talking about the weather in their hometowns.)

Wáng Yīng:　Nǐ jiāxiāng de tiānqì gēn zhèr　yíyàng ma?
王　英：你家乡的天气跟这儿一样吗？ comparison

Gāo Yīfēi:　Chàbuduō.　Dōngtiān hěn lěng,　wǒmen chángcháng qù huá xuě;
高一飞：差不多。冬天 很冷，我们 常常 去滑雪；

xiàtiān hěn rè,　wǒmen chángcháng qù yóu yǒng.　Nǐ jiāxiāng ne?
夏天很热，我们 常常 去游泳。你家乡呢？

Wáng Yīng:　Wǒ jiāxiāng de tiānqì　bǐ zhèr hǎo.　Wǒmen de dōngtiān bǐ zhèr　lái de
王　英：我家乡的天气比这儿好。我们 的冬天比这儿来得

wǎn,　wǒmen de chūntiān bǐ　zhèr　lái de zǎo.
晚，我们的春天比这儿来得早。 comparison

Gāo Yīfēi:　Yě jiù shì shuō,　dōngtiān bǐjiào duǎn.
高一飞：也就是说，冬天 比较 短。 restating

Wáng Yīng:　Yě méiyǒu zhème lěng.
王　英：也没有这么冷。

Gāo Yīfēi:　Xiàtiān ne?
高一飞：夏天呢？

Wáng Yīng:　Méiyǒu zhème rè.
王　英：没有这么热。 comparison

Gāo Yīfēi:　Shì ge　hǎo dìfang.
高一飞：是个好地方。

Wáng Yīng:　Shì a.　Nǐ zuì xǐhuan shénme　jìjié?
王　英：是啊。你最喜欢什么季节？

Gāo Yīfēi:　Qiūtiān.　Nà shíhou hěn shǎo xià yǔ,　yě bù guā fēng,　tiānqì

高一飞：秋天。那时候很少下雨，也不刮风，天气

hǎojí le.

好极了。

Wáng Yīng:　Wǒ gēn nǐ yíyàng,　yě xǐhuan qiūtiān. Nà shíhou,　wǒ jiāxiāng de fēngyè

王　英：我跟你一样，也喜欢秋天。那时候，我家乡的枫叶

dōu hóng le,　měijí le.

都红了，美极了。  [giving reasons]

## 注释　Zhùshì　**Notes**

美极了

   … 极了 is used in an exclamatory sentence to indicate a high degree.

# 5.3 Language Points

❀ Comparison

There are several ways to indicate comparison:

（1）A 跟 B 一样

他跟我一样高。He is as tall as me.

我跟你一样，也喜欢秋天。I'm the same as you. I like autumn too.

（2）A 比 B ……

This can be subdivided into the following types:

## A 比 B + Adj.

E.g. 他比我高。 He is taller than me.

我家乡的天气比这儿好。The weather in my hometown is better than here.

Attention: Logically the second example should be 我家乡的天气比这儿的天气好. But in the case with no ambiguity, the second 的天气 can be omitted. Another example is:

他的汉语比我流利。 His Chinese is more fluent than mine.

## A 比 B + Adj. 一点儿

E.g. 他比我高一点儿。 He is a bit taller than me.

昨天比今天冷一点儿。 It was a bit colder yesterday than today.

## A 比 B + Adj. 得多 / 多了

E.g. 他比我高得多。 He is much taller than me.

我家乡的夏天比这儿凉快多了。Summer in my hometown is much cooler than here.

Attention: If there is a big difference between the two things being compared, "A 比 B … 得多" or "A 比 B … 多了" should be used. The pattern "A 比 B 很/非常 … " is not correct.

## A 比 B + 更 / 还 Adj.

E.g.  他比我更高。He is even taller than me.

我家乡比这儿还热。It is even hotter in my hometown than here.

Attention: The comparative sentence A 比 B + 更/还 Adj. means "B is quite …, but A is even more …."

## A 比 B + V+ 得 + Adj.
## A +V 得 + 比 B + Adj.

E.g.  我们的冬天来得比这儿晚。/ 我们的冬天比这儿来得晚。

Winters in our hometown come later than here.

他（说汉语）说得比我好。/ 他（说汉语）比我说得好。

He speaks Chinese better than me.

（3）A 有 / 没有 B（这么 / 那么）+……

This can be subdivided into the following types:

## A 有 / 没有 B（这么 / 那么）+Adj.

E.g.  昨天没有今天这么冷。It was not as cold yesterday as it is today.

今天没有昨天那么暖和。It is not as warm today as it was yesterday.

## A + V. 得 + 有 / 没有 B（这么 / 那么）+ Adj.
## A+ 有 / 没有 B + V. 得 + （这么 / 那么）+ Adj.

E.g.  他（说汉语）说得没有我（这么）好。

他（说汉语）没有我说得（这么）好。

He does not speak Chinese as well as me.

⚙ According to the data provided in the boxes, compare the two situations in each group.

A

_____

_____

_____

| 小张 | 170cm | 小王 | 170cm |
| 今天 | 25℃ | 昨天 | 25℃ |
| 我 9:00 到学校 | | 他 9:00 到学校 | |

B

_____

_____

| 小张 170cm | 小李 172cm |
| 今天 25℃ | 前天 27℃ |
| 我 9:00 到学校 | 你 9:10 到学校 |

C

_____

_____

_____

| 小张 170cm | 小高 200cm |
| 今天 25℃ | 明天 35℃ |
| 我 9:00 到学校 | 老师 7:00 到学校 |

D

_____

_____

_____

| 小白 210cm | 小高 200cm |
| 后天 39℃ | 明天 35℃ |
| 校长 6:30 到学校 | 老师 7:00 到学校 |

 文化点 Wénhuàdiǎn Cultural notes

In China, the climate is varied and complex, because the country's large landmass includes five different climate zones: subarctic, temperate, warm-temperate, subtropical, and tropical zones. The landscape is quite varied. In addition, some regions are far away from the ocean, some are coastal, and still others are influenced by seasonal winds. All of these differences contribute to the complexity of China's climate. In Heilongjiang Province in the northeast, for example, the summers are short and not very hot, while the winters are long and severely cold. In Taiwan, Hainan, Guangdong, Guangxi, and Yunnan in the south, there are no winters; the weather is warm and rainy, and the trees are always green. In the middle and upper reaches of the Yangtze River and all along the Huai River, it is cold in the winter and hot in the summer; the four seasons are distinct. In the inland areas of the northwest, it is dry all year; there are sandstorms sometimes, and there is a great difference between daytime and night-time temperatures. On the Qinghai-Tibetan Plateau, the air is thin and the mountains are covered with snow throughout the year.

The following is a table of the average temperatures (˚C) and number of days with precipitation in the major cities of China:

| City | Jan | Feb | Mar | Apr | May | June | July | Aug | Sept | Oct | Nov | Dec |
|------|-----|-----|-----|-----|-----|------|------|-----|------|-----|-----|-----|
| Beijing | -4.7 | -2.3 | 4.4 | 13.2 | 20.2 | 24.2 | 26.0 | 24.6 | 19.5 | 12.5 | 4.0 | -2.8 |
|  | 2.1 | 3.1 | 4.5 | 5.1 | 6.4 | 9.7 | 14.5 | 14.1 | 6.9 | 5.0 | 3.6 | 1.6 |
| Harbin | -19.7 | -15.4 | -5.1 | 6.1 | 14.3 | 20.0 | 22.7 | 21.4 | 14.3 | 5.9 | -5.8 | -15.5 |
|  | 6.8 | 4.9 | 6.2 | 6.9 | 10.3 | 12.6 | 16.3 | 13.4 | 12.0 | 7.2 | 5.4 | 5.9 |
| Shanghai | 3.3 | 4.6 | 8.3 | 13.8 | 18.8 | 23.2 | 27.9 | 27.8 | 23.8 | 17.9 | 12.6 | 6.2 |
|  | 9.0 | 10.2 | 13.1 | 13.5 | 15.0 | 13.1 | 11.4 | 10.0 | 11.6 | 8.4 | 9.1 | 8.6 |

| City | Jan | Feb | Mar | Apr | May | June | July | Aug | Sept | Oct | Nov | Dec |
|------|-----|-----|-----|-----|-----|------|------|-----|------|-----|-----|-----|
| Guangzhou | 13.4 | 14.2 | 17.7 | 21.8 | 25.7 | 27.2 | 28.3 | 28.2 | 27.0 | 23.8 | 19.7 | 15.2 |
|  | 7.8 | 11.4 | 14.7 | 15.1 | 17.8 | 20.3 | 16.6 | 16.2 | 13.1 | 6.0 | 5.6 | 6.2 |
| Urumqi | -10.6 | -9.8 | -3.8 | 2.7 | 8.4 | 12.9 | 14.7 | 13.5 | 8.6 | 1.9 | -5.5 | -8.7 |
|  | 5.8 | 5.6 | 10.6 | 11.4 | 13.1 | 16.2 | 18.9 | 13.9 | 9.2 | 6.8 | 7.4 | 6.5 |
| Kunming | 7.8 | 9.8 | 13.2 | 16.7 | 19.3 | 19.5 | 19.9 | 19.2 | 17.6 | 15.0 | 11.5 | 8.3 |
|  | 4.1 | 3.9 | 5.0 | 5.5 | 11.4 | 18.9 | 21.3 | 21.1 | 15.2 | 16.1 | 6.9 | 4.6 |
| Taipei | 10.9 | 15.7 | 18.5 | 22.3 | 25.0 | 28.8 | 30.2 | 29.5 | 28.2 | 23.5 | 20.3 | 18.3 |
|  | 17 | 12 | 14 | 11 | 14 | 15 | 22 | 18 | 12 | 8 | 4 | 11 |

# Unit 6

## Wǒ Lǎojiā Zài Dōngběi
## 我 老家 在 东北
### My Hometown Is in the Northeast

## Learning objectives

* Expressing direction and location
* Talking about one's home and the environment
* Urban and rural areas

## Key sentences

Wo jiā běibian shì shān, nánbian shì hé.
我 家 北边 是 山 , 南边 是 河。
There's a mountain on the north side of my house and a river on the south side.

Nàr yídìng hěn rènao.
那儿 一定 很 热闹。
It must be very lively there.

Dàgài xūyào bàn gè xiǎoshí.
大概 需要 半 个 小时。
It takes about half an hour.

Nǐ jiā lí hǎi yuǎn ma?
你家 离 海 远 吗?
Is your home far from the sea?

# 6.1

Wǒ Jiā  Běibian Shì Shān，Nánbian Shì Hé

## 我家北边是山，南边是河

## There's a mountain on the north side of my house and a river on the south side

**Preliminary exercises**

1 Warm up

你知道中国的城市和农村有哪些不一样吗？

2 Learn the following words and form correct sentences with the words under the teacher's guidance.

（1）是  北方人  南方人  你  还是

（2）住在  城市  农村  你  喜欢  还是

（3）是  山  北边  我家，是  河  南边

（4）吵  市中心  太  了，疼  我  头

（5）车水马龙  市中心，热闹  极  了

（6）新鲜  优美  方便  交通  环境  空气  那儿

3 Fill in the blanks according to the recording.

（1）那儿_____很热闹吧？

（2）那儿_____不舒服！

（3）那儿_____是个好地方！

（4）那儿的环境美_____！

（5）那儿吵_____！

Question:

What words have we learned that can express the tone of the speaker?

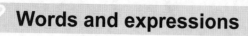

## Words and expressions

| | | | | |
|---|---|---|---|---|
| 1. | 老家 | ( N. ) | lǎojiā | hometown |
| 2. | 农村 | ( N. ) | nóngcūn | countryside |
| 3. | 北方 | ( LW ) | běifāng | north |
| 4. | 南方 | ( LW ) | nánfāng | south |
| 5. | 东北 | ( LW ) | dōngběi | northeast |
| 6. | 东边（东面） | ( LW ) | dōngbian (dōngmiàn) | east side |
| 7. | 南边（南面） | ( LW ) | nánbian (nánmiàn) | south side |
| 8. | 西边（西面） | ( LW ) | xībian (xīmiàn) | west side |
| 9. | 北边（北面） | ( LW ) | běibian (běimiàn) | north side |
| 10. | 对面 | ( LW ) | duìmiàn | opposite side |
| 11. | 河 | ( N. ) | hé | river |
| 12. | 空气 | ( N. ) | kōngqì | air |
| 13. | 环境 | ( N. ) | huánjìng | environment, surroundings |
| 14. | 交通 | ( N. ) | jiāotōng | transportation, traffic |
| 15. | 方便 | ( Adj. ) | fāngbiàn | convenient |
| 16. | 热闹 | ( Adj. ) | rènao | bustling with noise and excitement; lively |
| 17. | 吵 | ( Adj. ) | chǎo | noisy |
| 18. | 车水马龙 | | chēshuǐ-mǎlóng | heavy traffic |
| 19. | 一定 | ( Adv. ) | yídìng | surely, definitely |
| 20. | 多（么） | ( Adv. ) | duō (me) | how |
| 21. | 死 | ( V. ) | sǐ | die |

Listen to the dialogue and answer the following questions in Chinese.
（1）小张老家在哪儿？那里怎么样？。
（2）高一飞老家在哪儿？那里怎么样？

Listen to the recording while reading the text on the next page.

Read the text aloud and try not to look at the pinyin.

Work in groups and act out the conversation.

Activity
Discussion: In your opinion, is it better to live in the city or in the country?

## Vocabulary extension

| | | | | | | |
|---|---|---|---|---|---|---|
| 安静 | ānjìng | quiet | 污染 | wūrǎn | to pollute; pollution |
| 富 | fù | rich | 穷 | qióng | poor; impoverished |
| 居民 | jūmín | resident | 农民 | nóngmín | farmer |
| 落后 | luòhòu | fall behind | | | |
| 现代化 | xiàndàihuà | modernization | | | |
| 市区 | shìqū | the city proper; urban district | | | |
| 郊区 | jiāoqū | suburban district; suburbs | | | |

_____    _____

_____    _____

(Gao Yifei and Xiao Zhang are talking about their hometowns.)

Gāo Yīfēi:　Nǐ dàgài shì běifāngrén ba?
高一飞：你大概是北方人吧？

Xiǎo Zhāng:　Shì a, wǒ lǎojiā zài Dōngběi.
小　张：是啊，我老家在东北。

Gāo Yīfēi:　Nǐ jiā zài chéngshì háishi zài nóngcūn?
高一飞：你家在城市还是在农村？

Xiǎo Zhāng:　Zài nóngcūn. Wǒ jiā běibian shì shān, nánbian shì hé.
小　张：在农村。我家北边是山，南边是河。 [expressing location]

Gāo Yīfēi:　Kōngqì xīnxiān, huánjìng yōuměi, zhēn shì ge hǎo dìfang.
高一飞：空气新鲜，环境优美，真是个好地方。 [compliment]

Xiǎo Zhāng:　Hǎo shénme ya! Jiāotōng yìdiǎnr yě bù fāngbiàn. Nǐ jiā
小　张：好什么呀！交通一点儿也不方便。你家 [complaint]

yě zài nóngcūn ma?
也在农村吗？

Gāo Yīfēi:　Bù, wǒ jiā zài shì zhōngxīn.
高一飞：不，我家在市中心。

Xiǎo Zhāng:　Nàr yídìng hěn rènao.
小　张：那儿一定很热闹。 [supposition]

Gāo Yīfēi:　Shì a, wǒ jiā dōngbian, xībian yǒu hěn duō shāngdiàn, hái yǒu bù
高一飞：是啊，我家东边、西边有很多商店，还有不

shǎo fàndiàn, qiánmiàn shì mǎlù, cóng zǎo dào wǎn, chēshuǐ-mǎlóng.
少 饭店，前面是马路，从早到晚，车水马龙。

Xiǎo Zhāng: Nà duō hǎo wa!
小 张：那多 好哇!

Gāo Yìfēi: Hǎo shénme! Chǎosǐ le!
高一飞：好 什么! 吵死了!  [complaint]

 注释  Zhùshì  **Notes**

（一）我老家在东北

Note that the word order in Chinese directional expressions, 东北 (northeast), 东南 (southeast), 西北 (northwest), and 西南 (southwest), is opposite to that in English.

（二）好什么

This means "not good."

（三）那多好

How nice it is! 多（么）... is an exclamatory sentence that indicates a high degree.

（四）吵死了

... 死了 here is an exclamatory sentence that indicates a high degree.

# 6.2

Nǐ Jiā Lí Hǎi Yuǎn Ma?
## 你家离海远吗?
### Is your home far from the sea?

⬇ **Preliminary exercises**

1️⃣ **Warm up**
你家怎么样？大不大？
你每天怎么来学校的？

2️⃣ **Learn the following words and form correct sentences with the words under the teacher's guidance.**
（1）在 东部 西部 你 家 还是
（2）是 小楼 两 层 一 个 我 家
（3）有 树 花儿 很 多 院子 里 和
（4）去 散步 海边 我们 常常
（5）远 我 家 市中心 离 比较
（6）需要 半 个 小时 开 车 去 学校 从 我 家 大概

3️⃣ **Fill in the blanks according to the recording.**
（1）宿舍＿＿＿＿＿＿教室不太远。
（2）我常常＿＿＿＿＿我朋友一起去散步。
（3）＿＿＿＿＿星期一＿＿＿＿＿星期五我们都有课。
（4）＿＿＿＿＿前走，＿＿＿＿＿右拐，就到了。
（5）这些照片可以＿＿＿＿＿我看看吗?

Question:

What prepositions have we learned? Can you create a sentence using each of the prepositions?

**Words and expressions**

| 1. | 东部 | ( PW ) | dōngbù | east |
|---|---|---|---|---|
| 2. | 西部 | ( PW ) | xībù | west |
| 3. | 楼 | ( N. ) | lóu | building, floor |
| 4. | 层 | ( MW ) | céng | storey |
| 5. | 卧室 | ( N. ) | wòshì | bedroom |
| 6. | 客厅 | ( N. ) | kètīng | sitting room |
| 7. | 厨房 | ( N. ) | chúfáng | kitchen |
| 8. | 卫生间 | ( N. ) | wèishēngjiān | bathroom |
| 9. | 车库 | ( N. ) | chēkù | garage |
| 10. | 院子 | ( N. ) | yuànzi | yard |
| 11. | 树 | ( N. ) | shù | tree |
| 12. | 海 | ( N. ) | hǎi | sea |
| 13. | 海边 | ( PW ) | hǎibiān | seaside |
| 14. | 开 | ( V. ) | kāi | drive, open |
| 15. | 散步 | ( V.O. ) | sànbù | take a walk |
| 16. | 需要 | ( V. & N. ) | xūyào | to need; need |
| 17. | 小时 | ( N. ) | xiǎoshí | hour |

Unit
6

⚙ Listen to the dialogue and answer the following questions in Chinese.
（1）马丁的家在哪儿？他家有院子吗？院子里有什么？
（2）马丁每天怎么去学校？
（3）马丁什么时候去海边散步？一个人去吗？

⚙ Listen to the recording while reading the text on the next page.

⚙ Read the text aloud and try not to look at the pinyin.

⚙ Work in groups and act out the conversation.

⚙ Activity
Students: Tell your classmates about your house.

## Vocabulary extension

| 东方 | dōngfāng | the East, the Orient | 西方 | xīfāng | the West |
|------|----------|---------------------|------|--------|----------|
| 湖 | hú | lake | 草 | cǎo | grass |
| 森林 | sēnlín | forest | 沙漠 | shāmò | desert |
| 公寓 | gōngyù | apartment | 公园 | gōngyuán | park |
| 商业区 | shāngyèqū | business/commercial area | | | |
| 住宅区 | zhùzháiqū | residential quarters | | | |

_____        _____

_____        _____

**Text**

(Li Xiaoyu, Martin's language partner, is chatting with Martin today.)

Lǐ Xiǎoyǔ:　Nǐ jiā zài dōngbù háishi xībù?
李小雨：你家在东部还是西部？

Mǎdīng:　Wǒ jiā zài dōngbù.
马　丁：我家在东部。 〔expressing location〕

Lǐ Xiǎoyǔ:　Nǐ jiā dà bu dà?
李小雨：你家大不大？

Mǎdīng:　Bǐjiào dà.　Wǒ jiā shì yí gè liǎng céng xiǎo lóu,　yīcéng shì kètīng
马　丁：比较大。我家是一个两层小楼，一层是客厅

hé cāntīng,　èrcéng shì wòshì　Xiǎo lóu hòumiàn shì yí gè chēkù.
和餐厅，二层是卧室。小楼后面是一个车库。

Lǐ Xiǎoyǔ:　Nǐ jiā yǒu yuànzi ma?
李小雨：你家有院子吗？

Mǎdīng:　Yǒu.　Wǒ jiā qiánmiàn shì yí gè xiǎo yuànzi,　yuànzi li yǒu hěn duō
马　丁：有。我家前面是一个小院子，院子里有很多

shù hé huār.
树和花儿。 〔description〕

Lǐ Xiǎoyǔ:　Cóng nǐ jiā dào xuéxiào yuǎn bu yuǎn?
李小雨：从你家到学校远不远？

Mǎdīng:　Hái kěyǐ.　Wǒ měi tiān kāi chē qù xuéxiào,　dàgài xūyào bàn gè
马　丁：还可以。我每天开车去学校，大概需要半个

xiǎoshí.
小时。

Lǐ Xiǎoyǔ: Nǐ jiā lí hǎi yuǎn ma?
李小雨：你家离海远吗？

Mǎdīng: Bù yuǎn, wǒ chángcháng qù hǎibiān. Chīwán wǎnfàn, wǒ jiù gēn
马　丁：不远，我 常常 去海边。吃完 晚饭，我就跟

Ānnà yìqǐ qù hǎibiān sànbù.
安娜一起去海边散步。 description

Lǐ Xiǎoyǔ: Nǐ nǚpéngyou yě xǐhuan qù hǎibiān?
李小雨：你女朋友也喜欢去海边？

Mǎdīng: Nǚpéngyou? Shéi shì wǒ nǚpéngyou?
马　丁：女朋友？谁是我女朋友？ surprise

Lǐ Xiǎoyǔ: Ānnà bú shì nǐ de nǚpéngyou ma?
李小雨：安娜不是你的女朋友吗？

Mǎdīng: Bú shì. Ānnà shì wǒ de gǒu.
马　丁：不是。安娜是我的狗。

# 6.3 Language Points

❋ I. A Summary of Prepositions

The prepositions we have learned are:

在 从 到 离 给 往 跟 为 对

A preposition and a noun phrase together form a prepositional phrase, which is often used as an adverbial to modify a verb or an adjective. For example:

（1）你<u>在哪儿</u>工作？
（2）你<u>从哪儿</u>来？
（3）你<u>到哪儿</u>去？
（4）<u>从星期一到星期五</u>我们都上课。
（5）你家<u>离海边</u>远不远？
（6）请您<u>给我</u>买一张火车票，好吗？
（7）<u>往前</u>走，然后<u>往右</u>拐。（=<u>向前</u>走，然后<u>向右</u>拐。）
（8）我明天<u>跟朋友</u>一起去打球。
（9）这件礼物是<u>为你</u>买的。
（10）他<u>对北京</u>很熟悉。

❋ II. A Summary of Adverbs

The adverbs we have learned are:

不 没（有） 别
都 只 也 还
比较 很 非常 特别 最 更 还 有点儿
一定 可能 大概
刚 已经 再 常常 很少
就 真 多 太

Adverbs precede verbs or adjectives and indicate negation, range, degree, estimation, time, frequency, mood, etc. For example:

我没有时间，不想去了。/ 昨天我没有时间，没去。/ 你别去了吧。
他只会说汉语。/ 她会说汉语，他也会说汉语。/ 他们都会说汉语。/
他会说汉语，还会说日语。
今天有点儿热。/ 今天不太热。/ 今天很热。/ 今天比较热。/ 今天非常热。/ 今天特别热。/
今天是今年最热的一天。/ 今天比昨天更热。/ 今天比昨天还热。
现在他可能还在睡觉。/ 现在他大概还在睡觉。/ 现在他一定还在睡觉。

他刚回来。/ 他已经回来了。/ 他还没回来。
那儿常常下雨。/ 那儿很少下雨。
前面就是我家。
这儿真漂亮！/ 那多好哇！/ 太贵了！

⚙ Complete the following sentences using the adverb or preposition provided.

在 从 到 离 给 往 跟 比 对
（1）我_____这个地方不太熟悉。
（2）你_____哪儿来，要_____哪儿去？
（3）要是有空的话，请_____我打电话。
（4）他每天早上来得_____我一样早。

不 没 别 也 还 刚 已经 就
（1）你_____担心，我们会帮助你的。
（2）他_____起床，还_____吃早饭呢！
（3）11 月，南方还很暖和，北方_____下雪了。
（4）天气越热，去海边游泳的人_____越多。

## 文化点　Wénhuàdiǎn　Cultural notes

1. The majority of the Chinese population still lives in the countryside. After the economic reform and the opening-up of China, urban trade and labor markets have expanded rapidly. Many people from the countryside rushed into the cities to take advantage of new opportunities. Small and medium-sized cities, and new townships have rapidly developed, resulting in a significant percentage of the rural population becoming urbanized. In coastal areas, transportation has become more convenient in the countryside and industry has rapidly developed in the towns. Farmers' living standards have quickly improved so that the difference between city and country life has gradually lessened.

\*　　　\*　　　\*

2. Such sayings as, "chēshuǐ-mǎlóng" (incessant streams of horses and carriages; heavy traffic), are "chéngyǔ", or idioms, usually formed with four characters/syllables. Some idioms are very colloquial, such as: "rénshān-rénhǎi" (people mountain, people sea; huge crowds), "huāntiān-xǐdì" (sky-high joy, earth-wide glee; wild with joy), "qīshǒu-bājiǎo" (seven hands, eight feet; everyone lending a hand), "luànqī-bāzāo" (seven messy, eight chaos; at sixes and sevens). Some idioms have been passed down from ancient times and actually refer to classic stories, such as "kèzhōu-qiújiàn" (making a mark on the side of one's boat to indicate the place where one's sword has dropped into the river; to take measures without considering the changing circumstances); "hújiǎ-hǔwēi" (the fox borrows the tiger's fierceness; bullying people using someone else's power); "zìxiāngmáodùn" (bragging about one's impenetrable shields and all-penetrating spears; self-contradiction), and many others.

# Unit 7

## Wǒ Xuéguo Bàn Nián Hànyǔ
## 我 学过 半 年 汉语
## I Have Studied Chinese for Half a Year

## Learning objectives

* Expressing duration of time and times/frequency of actions
* Compliments and criticisms
* Learning a foreign language

## Key sentences

Wǒ xuéle liùnián Yīngyǔ le.

我 学了 六年 英语 了。

I've been studying English for six years now.

Nǐ kàn, wǒmen yí gè xīngqī jiàn jǐ cì miàn?

你看，我们 一个星期 见几次面？

How many times do you think we should meet each week?

Měi cì duō cháng shíjiān?

每次多 长 时间？

How long each time?

Hǎo, wǒ zài shuō yí biàn.

好，我 再 说 一 遍。

OK. I'll say it once again.

Nǐ ya, tài bù nǔlì le!

你呀，太不努力了！

You are not working hard enough!

# 7.1

Měi Cì Liànxí Liǎng Gè Xiǎoshí Hànyǔ

## 每 次练习两 个 小时 汉语

## Practice Chinese for two hours each time

## Preliminary exercises

1. **Warm up**

   你的专业是什么？

   你学了多长时间的汉语了？现在汉语学得怎么样？

2. Learn the following words and form correct sentences with the words under the teacher's guidance.

   （1）做 自我介绍 你 一 个 请

   （2）是 学生 专业 年级 我 经济 一

   （3）说 标准 普通话 你 得 很

   （4）想 练习 口语 我 跟 你 汉语

   （5）对不起，听 清楚 不太 得 我

   （6）还可以 口语 我 的，不太 好 阅读 写作 和

3. Choose the sentences that appear in the recording.

   （1）我学了半年汉语了。/ 我学汉语半年了。

   （2）我学过半个月汉语。/ 我学过汉语半个月。

   （3）我等了半个小时他。/ 我等了他半个小时。

   （4）我想每次练习汉语两个小时。/ 我想每次练习两个小时汉语。

   （5）我们一个星期见面几次？ / 我们一个星期见几次面？

   Question:

   What are the positions of words expressing duration of time or times/frequency of actions in sentences?

## Words and expressions

| | | | | |
|---|---|---|---|---|
| 1. | 自我 | ( Pron. ) | zìwǒ | oneself |
| 2. | 介绍 | ( V. & N. ) | jièshào | introduce; introduction |
| 3. | 专业 | ( N. ) | zhuānyè | major, specialty |
| 4. | 年级 | ( N. ) | niánjí | grade |
| 5. | 母语 | ( N. ) | mǔyǔ | mother tongue |
| 6. | 外语 | ( N. ) | wàiyǔ | foreign language |
| 7. | 外国 | ( N. ) | wàiguó | foreign country |
| 8. | 普通话 | ( N. ) | pǔtōnghuà | Mandarin |
| 9. | 听力 | ( N. ) | tīnglì | listening ability |
| 10. | 口语 | ( N. ) | kǒuyǔ | spoken language |
| 11. | 阅读 | ( N. & V. ) | yuèdú | reading; read |
| 12. | 写作 | ( N. & V. ) | xiězuò | writing; write |
| 13. | 标准 | ( Adj. & N. ) | biāozhǔn | standard; criterion |
| 14. | 清楚 | ( Adj. ) | qīngchu | clear |
| 15. | 练习 | ( V. & N. ) | liànxí | practice; exercise |
| 16. | 谈话 | ( V.O.) | tánhuà | talk |
| 17. | 互相 | ( Adv. ) | hùxiāng | each other |
| 18. | 年 | ( MW ) | nián | year |

Unit
7

⚙ Listen to the dialogue and answer the following questions in Chinese.

（1）陈静是谁？她为什么跟杰克见面？

（2）杰克是谁？他为什么跟陈静见面？

（3）他们打算一个星期见几次面？每次多长时间？

⚙ Listen to the recording while reading the text on the next page.

⚙ Read the text aloud and try not to look at the pinyin.

⚙ Work in groups and act out the conversation.

⚙ Activity

Students: How long have you been studying Chinese? How many Chinese classes do you have in a week? Do you practice and study Chinese every day? How long do you study for each day?

## Vocabulary extension

| | | | | | |
|---|---|---|---|---|---|
| 语音 | yǔyīn | pronunciation, phonetics | 词汇 | cíhuì | vocabulary |
| 语法 | yǔfǎ | grammar | 作业 | zuòyè | homework |
| 翻译 | fānyì | to translate; translation | 对话 | duìhuà | dialogue; to converse |
| 辅导 | fǔdǎo | to tutor | | | |
| 语言伙伴 | yǔyán huǒbàn | language partner | | | |

_____    _____

_____    _____

(Jack is in Beijing. He has found a language partner through a friend.)

Jiékè:　Nǐ hǎo,　wǒ xiān zìwǒ jièshào yíxià,　wǒ jiào Jiékè,　shì
杰　克：你好，我先自我介绍一下，我叫杰克，是　　　[introduction]

Jiānádàrén,　hěn gāoxìng rènshi nǐ. Wǒ xuéguo bàn nián Hànyǔ,
加拿大人，很高兴认识你。我学过半年汉语，

shuō de bú tài hǎo.
说得不太好。

Chén Jìng:　Nǐ shuō de búcuò.　Wǒ yě zìwǒ jièshào yíxià,　wǒ shì dàxué
陈　静：你说得不错。我也自我介绍一下，我是大学　　[introduction]

Yīngyǔ zhuānyè yī niánjí xuésheng, wǒ jiào Chén Jìng.　Wǒ xuéle
英语专业一年级学生，我叫陈静。我学了

liù nián Yīngyǔ le,　dànshì shuō de hěn bù hǎo.
六年英语了，但是说得很不好。

Jiékè:　Wǒ tīng wǒ péngyou shuō,　nǐ pǔtōnghuà shuō de hěn biāozhǔn,　Yīngyǔ
杰　克：我听我朋友说，你普通话说得很标准，英语

yě shuō de fēicháng liúlì.
也说得非常流利。　[compliment]

Chén Jìng:　Nǎli nǎli.　Wǒ de Yīngyǔ yuèdú hái kěyǐ,　tīnglì hé
陈　静：哪里哪里。我的英语阅读还可以，听力和　　[intention]

kǒuyǔ dōu bú tài hǎo,　xiězuò yě bù xíng. Suǒyǐ,　wǒ xiǎng zhǎo
口语都不太好，写作也不行。所以，我想找

Unit
7

yí wèi mǔyǔ shì Yīngyǔ de wàiguórén,　liànxí liànxí tīnglì
一位母语是英语的外国人，练习练习听力

hé kǒuyǔ.
和口语。

Jiékè:　Tài hǎo le!　Wǒ yě xiǎng liànxí liànxí wǒ de Hànyǔ tīnglì hé kǒuyǔ.
杰　克：太好了！我也想 练习练习我的汉语听力和口语。

Nǐ kàn,　wǒmen yí gè xīngqī jiàn jǐ cì miàn?
你看，我们一个星期见几次面？　opinion

Chén Jìng:　Sān cì ba.
陈　静：三次吧。

Jiékè:　Xíng.　Měi cì duō cháng shíjiān?
杰　克：行。每次多 长 时间？　opinion

Chén Jìng:　Měi cì liànxí liǎng gè xiǎoshí Yīngyǔ,　yí gè xiǎoshí Hànyǔ,　zěnmeyàng?
陈　静：每次练习两 个小时英语，一个小时汉语，怎么样？

Jiékè:　Shénme?　Wǒ tīng de bú tài qīngchu.　Nǐ shì bu shì shuō,　měi cì liànxí
杰　克：什么？我听得不太清楚。你是不是说，每次练习

liǎng gè xiǎoshí Hànyǔ,　yí gè xiǎoshí Yīngyǔ?　Nà hǎojí le!
两 个小时汉语，一个小时英语？那好极了！

# 7.2

Hǎo, Wǒ Zài Shuō Yí Biàn

## 好，我 再 说一遍

## OK. I'll say it once again

⬇ **Preliminary exercises**

**1** Warm up

汉语难学吗？

你觉得自己努力不努力？

**2** Learn the following words and form correct sentences with the words under the teacher's guidance.

（1）说 一点儿 慢 得 你 请

（2）开始 听写 我们 现在

（3）忘 我 这 个 汉字 的 意思 已经 了

（4）难 这 次 考试 很，好 不太 我 考 得

（5）快 你 说 得 太 了，糊里糊涂 我 听 得

（6）清楚 我 听 不太 得，说 再 一 遍 请 你

**3** Fill in the blanks according to the recording.

（1）我去过＿＿＿＿＿＿＿＿＿北京。

（2）我在他家吃过＿＿＿＿＿＿＿＿＿饭。

（3）对不起，请你再说＿＿＿＿＿＿＿＿＿。

（4）昨天晚上我听了＿＿＿＿＿＿＿＿＿录音。

（5）我们等他＿＿＿＿＿＿＿＿＿吧。

Question:

What are the differences between 次, 遍 and 下 ?

| | | | | |
|---|---|---|---|---|
| 1. | 食品 | ( N. ) | shípǐn | food |
| 2. | 句子 | ( N. ) | jùzi | sentence |
| 3. | 听写 | ( V. & N. ) | tīngxiě | dictate; dictation |
| 4. | 考试 | ( V.O. & N. ) | kǎoshì | (to) test |
| 5. | 开始 | ( V. ) | kāishǐ | begin |
| 6. | 结束 | ( V. ) | jiéshù | finish |
| 7. | 忘 | ( V. ) | wàng | forget |
| 8. | 慢 | ( Adj. ) | màn | slow |
| 9. | 努力 | ( Adj. ) | nǔlì | diligent |
| 10. | 难 | ( Adj. ) | nán | difficult |
| 11. | 容易 | ( Adj. ) | róngyì | easy |
| 12. | 糊里糊涂 | ( Adj. ) | húlihútu | muddled |
| 13. | 最后 | ( Adj. ) | zuìhòu | final |
| 14. | 分钟 | ( MW ) | fēnzhōng | minute |
| 15. | 刻钟 | ( MW ) | kèzhōng | quarter of an hour |
| 16. | 句 | ( MW ) | jù | measure word for sentences |
| 17. | 种 | ( MW ) | zhǒng | sort, kind |
| 18. | 遍 | ( MW ) | biàn | measure word for the repetition of the actions like reading, speaking, or writing |

☼ Listen to the dialogue and answer the following questions in Chinese.
(1) 老师让学生干什么？
(2) 老师的句子马丁听懂了没有？
(3) 马丁今天为什么有点糊里糊涂？

☼ Listen to the recording while reading the text on the next page.

☼ Read the text aloud and try not to look at the pinyin.

☼ Work in groups and act out the conversation.

☼ Activity
Students: What's the most difficult part of the Chinese language? How do you feel about this?

## Vocabulary extension

| | | | | | |
|---|---|---|---|---|---|
| 成绩 | chéngjì | score, grade, achievement | | | |
| 及格 | jígé | to pass (a test) | 通过 | tōngguò | to pass; go through |
| 学分 | xuéfēn | credit | 注册 | zhùcè | to register |
| 录音 | lùyīn | recording; to record | 水平 | shuǐpíng | level |
| 希望 | xīwàng | hope; to hope | 提高 | tígāo | to raise |

_____

_____

## Text

(In class, the teacher dictates sentences to the students as soon as class begins.)

Lǎoshī: Wǒmen xiān yòng shí fēnzhōng shíjiān tīngxiě jǐ gè jùzi, měi
老　师：我们先用十分钟 时间听写几个句子，每

gè jùzi wǒ zhǐ shuō sān biàn.
个句子我只说三遍。

Mǎdīng: Nán bu nán?
马　丁：难不难？

Lǎoshī: Hěn róngyì. Xiànzài kāishǐ. Dì-yī jù: Wǒmen qí zìxíngchē
老　师：很容易。现在开始。第一句：我们骑自行车

qù, wǒmen bú zuò qìchē qù.
去，我们不坐汽车去。

> making a request

Mǎdīng: Lǎoshī, nín shuō de tài kuài le, qǐng nín shuō de màn yìdiǎnr.
马　丁：老师，您说得太快了，请您说得慢一点儿。

Lǎoshī: Hǎo, wǒ zài shuō yí biàn: Wǒmen qí zìxíngchē qù, wǒmen bú zuò
老　师：好，我再说一遍：我们骑自行车去，我们不坐

qìchē qù.
汽车去。

> comprehension

Mǎdīng: Shénme yìsi? Wǒ tīng de bú tài qīngchu. Wǒmen … qí qìchē qù?
马　丁：什么意思？我听得不太清楚。我们……骑汽车去？

Lǎoshī: Xiànzài wǒ shuō zuìhòu yí biàn: Wǒmen qí zìxíngchē qù, wǒmen bú
老　师：现在我说最后一遍：我们骑自行车去，我们不

zuò qìchē qù.
坐汽车去。

Mǎdīng:     Tài nán le!      "Zìxíngchē"     shì shénme?

马　丁：太难了！"自行车"是什么？

Lǎoshī:     "Zìxíngchē",     wǒmen bú shì zǎo jiù xuéguo le ma?

老　师："自行车"，我们不是早就学过了吗？ reproach

Mǎdīng:     Duìbuqǐ,     wǒ wàng le.     Nà shì   yì zhǒng shípǐn ma?

马　丁：对不起，我忘了。那是一种食品吗？

Lǎoshī:     Nǐ ya,     tài bù nǔlì   le!

老　师：你呀，太不努力了！ reproach

Mǎdīng:     Lǎoshī,     bú shì wǒ bù nǔlì.     Zuótiān wǎnshang wǒ hē jiǔ   hēle   yí gè

马　丁：老师，不是我不努力。昨天晚上我喝酒喝了一个

duō xiǎoshí,     xiànzài hái yǒu diǎnr     húlihútu.

多小时，现在还有点儿糊里糊涂。

## 注释 Zhùshì Notes

（一）每个句子我只说三遍

　　遍 is similar to 次 in meaning. However, 遍 denotes the whole process of an action from beginning to end, and it is usually combined with 说, 听, 看, 写, etc.

（二）早就学过了

　　早就 means "already."

# 7.3 Language Points

## I. Expressions of Duration

| | |
|---|---|
| 一年 | a year |
| 一个月 | a month |
| 一天 | a day |
| 一（个）星期 | a week |
| 一（个）小时 | an hour |
| 一刻钟 | a quarter of an hour |
| 一分钟 | a minute |
| | |
| 半年 | half a year |
| 半个月 | half a month |
| 半天 | half a day |
| 半（个）星期 | half a week |
| 半（个）小时 | half an hour |
| 半分钟 | half a minute |
| | |
| 一年半 | a year and a half |
| 一个半月 | a month and a half |
| 一天半 | a day and a half |
| 一个半星期 | a week and a half |
| 一个半小时 | an hour and a half |

There are several patterns that are used to express the duration of an action:

> **V. + duration**
> **V. O. + V. + duration**

E.g. （1）我每天工作八个小时。
（2）我等了三个小时。
（3）我学汉语学了半年了。
（4）昨天晚上我喝酒喝了三个小时。

If the object of the verb is a noun, the expression of duration can be placed between the verb and the object. But if the object is a pronoun, the expression of duration must follow the object.

$$V. + duration + （的） + N.$$
$$V. + Pron. + duration$$

E.g.（1）我每天看三个小时（的）电视。

（2）我等了半个小时（的）公共汽车。

（3）我等了你半个小时了。

## II. Expressions for Times/Frequency of Action

The patterns expressing times/frequency of action are as follows:

$$V. + 【Num. + 次 / 遍】$$

E.g.（1）每个句子我只说三遍。

（2）他来过一次。

There are two cases when the verb is followed by an object: if the object is a noun, the expression of times/frequency precedes the object; and if the object is a pronoun, the expression of times/frequency follows the object.

$$V. + 【Num. + 次 / 遍】 + N.$$
$$V. + Pron. + 【Num. + 次 / 遍】$$

E.g.（1）我在他家吃过三次饭。

（2）我听了三遍录音。

（3）我去过那儿两次。

However, if the object is a proper noun (the name of a person or a place), either pattern may be used, for example:

（1）我问过两次杰克。/ 我问过杰克两次。

（2）我去过两次北京。/ 我去过北京两次。

Choose the correct sentence in each group.

（1）A. 我们每天工作八小时。

B. 我们每天八小时工作。

C. 我们八小时每天工作。

（2）A. 我等公共汽车等了一刻钟。

B. 我等了公共汽车一刻钟。

C. 我一刻钟等了公共汽车。

（3）A. 我每天上两个小时网。

B. 我每天上网两个小时。

C. 我每天两个小时上网。

（4）A. 我见过他一次。

B. 我见过一次他。

C. 我一次见过他。

文化点　Wénhuàdiǎn　**Cultural notes**

1. The traditional reply to a compliment or to words of praise is, "Nǎli, nǎli" (No, not at all), because it is customary to deny that one deserves the compliment. Even if one is actually in complete agreement with the compliment, one must outwardly appear very modest and insist that one still has many inadequacies. This polite, self-depreciating behavior is called "kèqi." In modern society, the young tend not to act so modestly. They may just make a straightforward reply, like "Thank you," to a compliment. They may also subtly say, "Hái kěyǐ" (I guess I'm all right), meaning "I'm really pretty good."

\*　　　\*　　　\*

2. The Chinese pay much attention to the learning of foreign languages. The most widely studied language is English. English is universally taught in high schools. And in large cities, English instruction begins at the elementary level, continuing all the way up through university and graduate school. Foreign language courses are considered to be a standard part of school and university curricula.

# Unit 8

## Huǒchēpiào Màiwán Le
## 火车票　卖完　了
## The Train Tickets Are Sold Out

## Learning objectives

* Expressing actions and their result
* Expressing the continuation of actions or states
* Adjusting plans and solving problems
* Narrating a specific sequence of events

## Key sentences

Xīngqī'èr de huǒchēpiào yǐjīng màiwán le.
星期二的 火车 票 已经 卖完了。

The train tickets for Tuesday are sold out.

Xīngqīsān de cānguān huódòng dōu yǐjīng ānpái hǎo le.
星期三 的 参观 活动 都 已经 安排 好 了。

Wednesday's activities have already been scheduled.

Mǎidào yǐhòu qǐng nín gěi wǒ fā yí gè duǎnxìn.
买 到 以后 请 您 给 我 发 一 个 短信。

Please send me a text message when you get the ticket.

Tā qí de hěn kuài, yòushǒu hái názhe dōngxi.
他 骑 得 很 快， 右手 还 拿着 东西。

He rode very fast, with something in his right hand.

Wǒmen dōu shuāidǎo le.
我们 都 摔 倒 了。

We both fell down.

Unit
8

# 8.1

Huódòng Dōu Yǐjīng Ānpái Hǎo Le

## 活动 都 已经 安排 好 了

# All the activities have already been scheduled

---

## Preliminary exercises

1 Warm up

你在中国坐过火车或者飞机吗?

你觉得在中国坐火车方便还是坐飞机方便?

2 Learn the following words and form correct sentences with the words under the teacher's guidance.

（1）想 请 吃个饭 我们 领导 您

（2）打通 电话 没，发 短信 个 给 他 吧

（3）去 参观 金融 贸易 中心 我们 马上

（4）安排好 参观 活动 明天 都 已经 了 的

（5）对 感兴趣 我们 公司 老总 中国 市场 很

（6）因为 天气 原因，推迟 起飞 本次 航班

3 Fill in the blanks according to the recording.

（1）电话没有_____。

（2）车票_____了，我没有_____。

（3）明天的参观活动都_____了。

（4）今天下午的活动_____下星期三。

Question:

What similarities do the added words have in terms of sentence structure?

**Words and expressions**

| 1. | 金融 | ( N. ) | jīnróng | finance |
|---|---|---|---|---|
| 2. | 贸易 | ( N. ) | màoyì | trade |
| 3. | 外贸 | ( N. ) | wàimào | foreign trade |
| 4. | 市场 | ( N. ) | shìchǎng | market |
| 5. | 领导 | ( N. & V. ) | lǐngdǎo | leader; lead |
| 6. | 经理 | ( N. ) | jīnglǐ | manager |
| 7. | 手机 | ( N. ) | shǒujī | cell phone |
| 8. | 短信 | ( N. ) | duǎnxìn | short message (by cell phones) |
| 9. | 接 | ( V. ) | jiē | pick up (sb.); answer (the phone) |
| 10. | 通 | ( V. ) | tōng | get through; pass |
| 11. | 推迟 | ( V. ) | tuīchí | postpone |
| 12. | 安排 | ( V. & N. ) | ānpái | arrange; arrangement |
| 13. | 访问 | ( V. ) | fǎngwèn | visit |
| 14. | 参加 | ( V. ) | cānjiā | attend; take part in |
| 15. | 航班 | ( N. ) | hángbān | flight number |
| 16. | 马上 | ( Adv. ) | mǎshàng | at once; soon |
| 17. | 这样 | ( Pron. ) | zhèyàng | like this; in this way; thus |

Unit
**8**

⚙ Listen to the dialogue and answer the following questions in Chinese.
（1）杰克下星期二能不能到？为什么？
（2）下星期三，小黄为杰克安排了哪些活动？
（3）杰克马上去买什么？

⚙ Listen to the recording while reading the text on the next page.

⚙ Read the text aloud and try not to look at the pinyin.

⚙ Work in groups and act out the conversation.

⚙ Activity
Skit: (1) Jack is buying a train ticket for Beijing to Shanghai on the morning August 13;
(2) Jack is buying a plane ticket for Beijing to Shanghai on the morning of August 12.
After that, Jack will call Xiao Huang.

## Vocabulary extension

| | | | | | |
|---|---|---|---|---|---|
| 软座 | ruǎnzuò | soft seat | 硬座 | yìngzuò | hard seat |
| 软卧 | ruǎnwò | soft sleeper | 硬卧 | yìngwò | hard sleeper |
| 头等座 | tóuděngzuò | first class seat | 车次 | chēcì | train number |
| 商务舱 | shāngwùcāng | business class cabin | 经济舱 | jīngjìcāng | economy class cabin |
| 接待 | jiēdài | to receive (somebody) | 合作 | hézuò | to cooperate; cooperation |
| ____ | | ____ | ____ | | ____ |
| ____ | | ____ | ____ | | ____ |

(Jack is going to leave Beijing to go somewhere to discuss a joint venture with a certain company. Currently, Xiao Huang, the local person who will receive Jack, is calling to confirm the details of the journey.)

Xiǎo Huáng:　Shì Jiékè　ma?
小　黄：是杰克吗?

Jiékè:　Duì,　shì wǒ.
杰　克：对，是我。

Xiǎo Huáng:　Wǒ shì Xiǎo Huáng. Zuótiān gěi nín dǎle　jǐ　cì diànhuà,　dōu méi dǎtōng.
小　黄：我是小　黄。昨天给您打了几次电话，都 没 打通。

Nín xià　xīngqī'èr dào méiyǒu wèntí　ba?
您下星期二到 没有问题吧? 〔 certainty 〕

Jiékè:　Kànlái bù xíng le,　yào tuīchí dào xīngqīsān.　Xīngqī'èr de huǒchē-
杰　克：看来不行了，要推迟到星期三。星期二的火车

piào yǐjīng màiwán le.
票已经卖完了。

Xiǎo Huáng:　Kěshì,　xīngqīsān de cānguān huódòng dōu yǐjīng　ānpái hǎo le.
小　黄：可是，星期三的参观　活动 都已经安排好了。

Jiékè:　Yǒu xiē shénme huódòng?
杰　克：有些什么活动?

Xiǎo Huáng:　Shàngwǔ cānguān jīnróng màoyì zhōngxīn,　xiàwǔ　qù shìchǎng kànkan,
小　黄：上午 参观 金融贸易中心，下午去市场 看看，

wǎnshang wǒmen lǐngdǎo qǐng nín chīfàn,　jǐ jiā　wàimào gōngsī de
晚上我们 领导 请您吃饭，几家外贸公司的

jīnglǐ　yě　cānjiā.
经理也参加。

Unit
8

Jiékè: Nàme, wǒ bú zuò huǒchē le, wǒ zuò fēijī. Wǒ mǎshàng qù
杰 克：那么，我不坐火车了，我坐飞机。我马上去

mǎi xià xīngqī'èr de fēijīpiào.
买下星期二的飞机票。 ︹decision︺

Xiǎo Huáng: Mǎidào yǐhòu qǐng nín gěi wǒ fā yí gè duánxìn, gàosu wǒ nín de
小 黄：买到以后请您给我发一个短信，告诉我您的

hángbān. Wǒmen qù jiē nín.
航班。我们去接您。

Jiékè: Méi wèntí. Xièxie nǐ!
杰 克：没问题。谢谢你!

Xiǎo Huáng: Nà hǎo, jiù zhèyàng. Zàijiàn!
小 黄：那好，就这样。再见! ︹closing a conversation︺

 注释 Zhùshì Notes

看来不行了
　看来 denotes an air of evaluation.

# 8.2

Wǒmen Dōu Shuāidǎo Le

# 我们 都 摔倒 了

## We both fell down

## Preliminary exercises

**1** Warm up

你骑自行车吗？

你发生过交通事故吗？

**2** Learn the following words and form correct sentences with the words under the teacher's guidance.

（1）修 好 自行车 还 没

（2）发生 事故 交通 一 个 昨天 了

（3）小心 要 过 马路 的时候

（4）穿 雨衣 他 没，打 雨伞 没 也

（5）撞 行人 一 个 他 上班 路上 的 了

（6）摔 坏 他的 眼镜 了，摔 破 衣服 也 了

**3** Fill in the blanks according to the recording.

（1）房间里有的人坐_____，有的人站_____。

（2）他穿_____一件红衬衫。

（3）他手里拿_____一个杯子。

（4）房间的门开_____，可是里面没人。

Question:

What are the meanings of 着 in the above sentences?

Unit

8

## Words and expressions

| | | | | |
|---|---|---|---|---|
| 1. | 怎么回事 | | zěnme huí shì | what's the matter |
| 2. | 上班 | ( V.O. ) | shàngbān | go to work |
| 3. | 发生 | ( V. ) | fāshēng | happen; take place |
| 4. | 事故 | ( N. ) | shìgù | accident |
| 5. | 警察 | ( N. ) | jǐngchá | police, policeman |
| 6. | 雨衣 | ( N. ) | yǔyī | raincoat |
| 7. | 雨伞 | ( N. ) | yǔsǎn | umbrella |
| 8. | 手 | ( N. ) | shǒu | hand |
| 9. | 背 | ( N. ) | bèi | back |
| 10. | 结果 | ( N. ) | jiéguǒ | result |
| 11. | 检查 | ( V. ) | jiǎnchá | check |
| 12. | 修 | ( V. ) | xiū | repair |
| 13. | 撞 | ( V. ) | zhuàng | bump against; collide |
| 14. | 摔 | ( V. ) | shuāi | fall |
| 15. | 倒 | ( V. ) | dǎo | fall down |
| 16. | 伤 | ( V. & N. ) | shāng | to hurt; injury, wound |
| 17. | 坏 | ( Adj. ) | huài | bad, broken |
| 18. | 破 | ( Adj. ) | pò | broken |
| 19. | 着 | ( Part. ) | zhe | used to indicate the continuation of a state |

⚙ Listen to the dialogue and answer the following questions in Chinese.

（1）路上发生了什么事？

（2）里奇为什么没有看见行人？行人为什么也没有看见里奇？

（3）结果怎么样？

⚙ Listen to the recording while reading the text on the next page.

⚙ Read the text aloud and try not to look at the pinyin.

⚙ Work in groups and act out the conversation.

⚙ Activity

Discussion: Who is responsible for this accident?

**Unit 8**

## Vocabulary extension

| | | | | | | |
|---|---|---|---|---|---|---|
| 小心 | xiǎoxīn | careful(ly) | | 责任 | zérèn | responsibility |
| 遵守 | zūnshǒu | to obey | | 违反 | wéifǎn | to disobey |
| 规则 | guīzé | rule | | 停下来 | tíng xiàlai | to stop |
| 红绿灯（交通灯） | hónglǜdēng(jiāotōngdēng) | traffic lights | | | | |
| 闯红灯 | chuǎng hóngdēng | run the red traffic light | | | | |

_____    _____

_____    _____

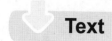 

(On his way to school, Richie accidentally knocks down a pedestrian. A policeman has just arrived.)

Jǐngchá:    Zěnme huí shì?
警　察：怎么回事？    asking for information

Xíngrén:    Tā zhuàngle wǒ.
行　人：他撞了我。

Jǐngchá:    Nǐ qí chē de shíhou méi kàndào tā yào guò mǎlù ma?
警　察：你骑车的时候没看到她要过马路吗？

Lǐqí:    Wǒ chuānzhe yǔyī,    méi kàn qīngchu.
里　奇：我穿着雨衣，没看清楚。

Xíngrén:    Tā qí de hěn kuài,    yòushǒu hái názhe dōngxi.
行　人：他骑得很快，右手还拿着东西。    description

Jǐngchá:    Nǐ guò mǎlù de shíhou,    méi kànjiàn tā qí zìxíngchē guòlai ma?
警　察：你过马路的时候，没看见他骑自行车过来吗？

Xíngrén:    Wǒ dǎzhe yǔsǎn,    méi kàn qīngchu.
行　人：我打着雨伞，没看清楚。

Jǐngchá:    Jiéguǒ ne?
警　察：结果呢？    asking for information

Lǐqí, xíngrén:    Wǒmen dōu shuāidǎo le.
里奇、行人：我们都摔倒了。

Lǐqí:    Wǒ de zìxíngchē shuāihuài le.
里　奇：我的自行车摔坏了。

行　人：Xíngrén: Wǒ de yǎnjìng shuāipò le.
我的眼镜摔破了。

警　察：Jǐngchá: Shuāishāngle méiyǒu?
摔伤了 没有？

行　人：Xíngrén: Bù zhīdào. Bèi shang yǒudiǎnr téng.
不知道。背 上 有点儿疼。

警　察：Jǐngchá: Zhèyàng ba, (to Richie) nǐ péi tā qù yīyuàn jiǎnchá yíxià
这样吧，(to Richie) 你陪她去医院检查一下 ··· decision

shēntǐ. (to the pedestrian) Jiǎnchá wán yǐhòu, nǐ péi tā qù xiū
身体。(to the pedestrian) 检查完以后，你陪他去修

zìxíngchē.
自行车。

行　人：Xíngrén: Kěshì, wǒ yào qù shàngbān…
可是，我要去 上班……

里　奇：Lǐqí: Wǒ yào qù shàngkè…
我要去上课……

警　察：Jǐngchá: Nà nǐmen jiù —
那你们就——

里奇、行人：Lǐqí, xíngrén: Zàijiàn ba!
再见吧！

## 注释　Zhùshì　Notes

（一）你骑车的时候没看到她要过马路吗

……的时候 means "when …." Other examples: 考试的时候可以看词典吗？ / 在北京旅行的时候，他拍了很多照片。 / 我们到他家的时候，他正在吃饭。

（二）这样吧

这样吧 indicates a solution arising from the deliberation of a difficult situation.

# 8.3 Language Points

## ❋ I. V./Adj. + Resultative Complement

A verb or an adjective which is directly placed after another verb or adjective to indicate result is called a resultative complement. The combination of verb and resultative complement is very flexible, but once the V.-Comple. construction is formed, its elements are bound closely together. The V.-Comple. is equivalent to a verb, and it can be followed by 了, 过 and an object.

E.g.　　他摔倒了。/ 他摔伤了。/ 衣服摔破了。/ 自行车摔坏了。

　　　　自行车摔坏了。/ 电话用坏了。/ 衣服穿坏了。/ 肚子吃坏了。

　　　　他撞倒了一个行人。/ 我没买到火车票。

The negative form is commonly "没（有）V.Comple." and the interrogative pattern is "V.Comple. 了吗，" "V.Comple.（了）没有" or "V. (Comple.) 没 V.Comple."

For example:　电话没打通。

　　　　　　　你摔伤了没有？/ 你摔（伤）没摔伤?

Here are some commonly used resultative complements:

1. 完

This indicates the fulfilment of an action so that nothing remains.

（1）我说完了。

（2）票卖完了。

2. 好

This indicates the fulfilment of an action, or that the result of the action is perfect.

（1）练习还没做好。

（2）门没关好。

3. 到

This indicates the action has reached its goal up to a certain point.

（1）词典没买到。

（2）今天早上我看到他了。

（3）汽车开到学校门口。

（4）昨天上到第八课。

（5）晚上看书看到十一点。

4. 见（"看见" see、"听见" hear）

（1）这几天你看见过他吗？

（2）你说什么？我没听见。

## II. V. + 着 (zhe)

着 attached to a verb indicates either (1) the action is in progress, or (2) the action is completed, but its consequences still linger on.

E.g. （1）你手里拿着什么？

（2）房间里有的人站着，有的人坐着。

（3）她穿着一件红衬衫，戴着一副眼镜。

（4）房间的门开着，可是里边没有人。

Complete the following sentences using resultative complements.

（1）他正在吃早饭，还没吃_____。

（2）电话没打_____，他关机了。

（3）车票已经卖_____了，我没有买_____。

（4）你说什么？我没听_____。能不能再说一遍？

（5）昨天晚上我们一起看电视看_____了十二点。

（6）那本书我朋友想看，我就借_____他了。

## 文化点　Wénhuàdiǎn　Cultural notes

China's economic reform and its opening-up started in 1978. The main objectives of this reform are: to establish special economic zones and economic development zones, to expand international exchange and cooperation, and to attract foreign investment and advanced technology. The appearance of the three-capital enterprises (foreign capital enterprises, joint venture enterprises and equity joint venture enterprises) has created a positive effect on China's economic development.

\* \* \* \*

Chinese trains are divided according to their speed into various classes, identified with different letters and numbers. The letters refer to different classes:

G　gāotiě

High-Speed Electric Multiple Unit (EMU) Train.

The top speed of which may reach 300km/h.

D　dòngchē

Electric Multiple Unit (EMU).

The designed top speed is 250km/h.

Z　zhídá lièchē

Direct Express

With a top speed of 160km/h, they run directly to the destination or have only a few stops on the way.

T tèkuài

Express

The highest speed is 140km/h. Almost every T-series is equipped with a soft sleeper, soft seat, hard sleeper and hard seat.

K kuàichē

Fast

This series with a top speed of 120km/h has more stops than the T trains. They are equipped with air-conditioning and the four classes of berths.

Train tickets can be purchased online or at designated ticket offices. There is a real-name policy when purchasing the ticket; you need to show your ID or passport.

# Unit 9

## Xiànzài Jiù Kěyǐ Bān Jìnqù
## 现在 就可以 搬 进去
## You Can Move in Right Away

## Learning objectives

✱ Expressing the direction of actions and the movements of objects

✱ Expressing complaints, discontent and urging somebody to do something

✱ Renting an apartment

### Key sentences

Rúguǒ nǐmen xiǎng zū dehuà , xiànzài jiù kěyǐ bān jìnqù.
如果 你们 想 租 的话， 现在 就可以 搬 进去。

If you want to rent it, you can move in right now.

Měi tiān zǒushàng zǒuxià, tài lèi le.
每 天 走 上 走 下，太累了。

It's very tiring to walk upstairs and downstairs every day.

Zhè hétong wǒmen kěyǐ dài huíqù kànkan ma?
这 合同 我们可以带 回去 看看 吗?

Can we take this contract to look over before signing?

Máfan nín kuài diǎnr mǎilái zhuāng shàngqù.
麻烦 您 快 点儿 买来 装 上去。

Please buy and install it soon.

## 9.1

Hétong Wǒmen Kěyǐ Dài Huíqù Kànkan Ma?

合同 我们 可以带回去 看看 吗？

## Can we take this contract back for a look?

**↓ Preliminary exercises**

1　Warm up

你知道吗，在中国的大城市，人们一般住多大的房子？租一套公寓大概要多少钱？

2　Learn the following words and form correct sentences with the words under the teacher's guidance.

（1）住　在　六　楼　他

（2）付　押金　先　请

（3）坐　上去　我们　电梯　吧

（4）锻炼　他　身体　每天　早上

（5）租　公寓　一　套　我　想，去　签　合同　明天

（6）新　是　冰箱　洗衣机　和　房间　里　的　都　的

3　Fill in the blanks according to the recording.

（1）每天得＿＿＿＿＿＿＿＿＿，太累了。

（2）我们＿＿＿＿＿＿＿＿＿休息一下吧。

（3）他从包里＿＿＿＿＿＿＿＿＿一份合同。

（4）他从国外＿＿＿＿＿＿＿＿＿很多礼物送给我们。

Question:

What special qualities do the added words have in terms of sentence structure?

## Words and expressions

| | | | | |
|---|---|---|---|---|
| 1. | 房子 | ( N. ) | fángzi | house |
| 2. | 公寓 | ( N. ) | gōngyù | apartment |
| 3. | 套 | ( MW ) | tào | a set of |
| 4. | 出租 | ( V. ) | chūzū | rent out |
| | 租 | ( V. ) | zū | rent |
| 5. | 签 | ( V. ) | qiān | sign, write |
| 6. | 合同 | ( N. ) | hétong | contract |
| 7. | 付 | ( V. ) | fù | pay |
| 8. | 押金 | ( N. ) | yājīn | deposit |
| 9. | 带 | ( V. ) | dài | take, bring, carry |
| 10. | 搬 | ( V. ) | bān | move |
| 11. | 锻炼 | ( V. ) | duànliàn | exercise; do physical training |
| 12. | 累 | ( Adj. ) | lèi | tired |
| 13. | 楼 | ( N. ) | lóu | building; storey, floor |
| 14. | 电梯 | ( N. ) | diàntī | elevator |
| 15. | 电视机 | ( N. ) | diànshìjī | TV set |
| 16. | 电冰箱 | ( N. ) | diànbīngxiāng | refrigerator |
| 17. | 洗衣机 | ( N. ) | xǐyījī | washing machine |

Unit
9

⚙ Listen to the dialogue and answer the following questions in Chinese.

（1）张园园和王英要租的房子在几楼？怎么上去？

（2）这套房子有几个房间？里面有一些什么电器？

（3）租金多少？

⚙ Listen to the recording while reading the text on the next page.

⚙ Read the text aloud and try not to look at the pinyin.

⚙ Work in groups and act out the conversation.

⚙ Activity

Students: What requirements do you have in renting an apartment; size, amenities, location etc.?

## Vocabulary extension

| | | | | | |
|---|---|---|---|---|---|
| 要求 | yāoqiú | demand, requirments | 广告 | guǎnggào | advertisement |
| 做饭 | zuòfàn | cooking | 微波炉 | wēibōlú | microwave oven |
| 邻居 | línjū | neighbor | 电费 | diànfèi | electricity fee |
| 洗 | xǐ | to wash | 洗澡 | xǐzǎo | take a bath |
| 电器 | diànqì | electrical appliances | 机器 | jīqi | machine |
| 份 | fèn | a set; measure word for items like documents | | | |

_____     _____

_____     _____

(Wang Ying and Zhang Yuanyuan want to rent an apartment together. Today they have found a place through an advertisement. They are now meeting the landlady, Mrs. Qian.)

Wáng Yīng:　Tīngshuō nín de　fángzi yào chūzū?
王　英：听说 您的 房子 要 出租?

Qián Tàitai:　Shìde.　　Nǐmen xiǎng zū dehua,　xiànzài jiù　kěyǐ　bān jìnqù.
钱太太：是的。 你们 想 租 的话, 现在 就 可以 搬进去。

Wáng Yīng:　Zài jǐ lóu?
王　英：在 几楼?

Qián Tàitai:　Liù lóu.　Shàngqù kànkan ba?
钱太太：六楼。 上去 看看 吧?　　suggestion

Wáng Yīng:　Yǒu méiyǒu diàntī?
王　英：有 没有 电梯?

Qián Tàitai:　Méiyǒu,　děi zǒu shàngqù.
钱太太：没有, 得 走上去。

Zhāng Yuányuan:　Měi tiān zǒushàng zǒuxià,　　tài lèi le.
张　园园：每天 走上 走下, 太累了。

Qián Tàitai:　Méi guānxi,　hái　kěyǐ duànliàn shēntǐ ne!
钱太太：没关系, 还可以 锻炼 身体 呢!　　reassurance

　　　　　　　　　　　Qǐng jìn ba.
(arriving at the sixth floor) 请 进吧。

Zhāng Yuányuan:　Zhè tào fángzi　yí gè　yuè duōshao qián?
张　园园：这套 房子 一个 月 多少 钱?

Qián Tàitai: Sānqiān kuài.
钱太太：三千块。

Wáng Yīng: Tài guì le!
王 英：太贵了！

Qián Tàitai: Yìdiǎnr yě bú guì. Nǐ kàn, zhè tào fángzi yǒu liǎng gè dà fángjiān.
钱太太：一点儿也不贵。你看，这套房子有 两 个大房间。

Diànshìjī, diànbīngxiāng, xǐyījī, diànhuà, dōu yǒu.
电视机、电冰箱、洗衣机、电话，都有。

Zhāng Yuányuan: Yào fù yājīn ma?
张 园园：要付押金吗？

Qián Tàitai: Fù sān qiān kuài yājīn, bān chūqù de shíhou huán gěi nǐ. Zhè shì
钱太太：付三千块押金，搬出去的时候还给你。这是

hétong.
合同。

hesitation

Wáng Yīng: Ǹg… wǒmen huíqù xiǎngxiang ba, míngtiān dǎ diànhuà gàosu nǐ.
王 英：嗯……我们回去 想想 吧，明天 打电话告诉你。

Zhè hétong wǒmen kěyǐ dài huíqù kànkan ma?
这合同我们可以带回去看看吗？

Qián Tàitai: Dāngrán kěyǐ. Míngtiān wǒ děng nǐmen de diànhuà.
钱太太：当然可以。明天 我 等你们的电话。

## 注释　Zhùshì　Notes

现在就可以搬进去

就 indicates that something happened or will happen right away. Here, it means "at once."

# 9.2

Máfan Nín Kuàidiǎnr Mǎilái Zhuāng Shàngqù
## 麻烦 您 快点儿 买来 装 上去
### Please buy and install it soon

⬇ **Preliminary exercises**

1 Warm up

你常常生气吗？生气的时候说什么？

2 Learn the following words and form correct sentences with the words under the teacher's guidance.

（1）生 气 谁 的 在 他 呢

（2）不像话 这 个 人 太 了

（3）拆 这些 旧 房子 什么时候

（4）装上 电脑 我 的 中文 软件 (ruǎnjiàn, software) 还没有

（5）陪 一起 去 没有 人 我，去 只好 我 一个人 了

（6）旧 这 台 冰箱 太 了，没 办法 修 已经 了

3 Fill in the blanks according to the recording.

（1）他从包里拿_____一本词典_____。

（2）他气得说不_____一句话_____。

（3）这份合同我可以带_____家_____吗？

（4）我看见她走_____房间_____了。

Question:

In the above sentences, what are the positions of the directional complements and the objects?

3（1）他从包里拿出来一本词典看。
（2）他气得说不出来一句话来。
（3）这份合同我可以带回家去吗？
（4）我看见她走进房间去了。

Listening script

## Words and expressions

| | | | | |
|---|---|---|---|---|
| 1. | 生气 | ( V.O. & Adj. ) | shēngqì | be angry; annoyed |
| 2. | 不像话 | ( Adv. ) | búxiànghuà | unreasonably |
| 3. | 电器 | ( N. ) | diànqì | electrical appliances |
| 4. | 空调 | ( N. ) | kōngtiáo | air conditioner, air-conditioning |
| 5. | 台 | ( MW ) | tái | measure word for appliances and machines |
| 6. | 旧 | ( Adj. ) | jiù | old |
| 7. | 拆 | ( V. ) | chāi | remove |
| 8. | 装 | ( V. ) | zhuāng | install |
| 9. | 送 | ( V. ) | sòng | send |
| 10. | 如果 | ( Conj. ) | rúguǒ | if |
| 11. | 房东 | ( N. ) | fángdōng | landlord, landlady, owner |
| 12. | 师傅 | ( N. ) | shīfu | technician; master worker |
| 13. | 办法 | ( N. ) | bànfǎ | way, method |
| 14. | 只好 | ( Adv. ) | zhǐhǎo | have to; be forced to |
| 15. | 一……就…… | | yī … jiù … | as soon as …; once … |
| 16. | 嘛 | ( Part. ) | ma | used to intensify the tone of a piece of advice or a request |

⚙ Listen to the dialogue and answer the following questions in Chinese.
    （1）张园园和王英为什么生气？
    （2）房东打算怎么办？
    （3）张园园和王英希望房东怎么样？

⚙ Listen to the recording while reading the text on the next page.

⚙ Read the text aloud and try not to look at the pinyin.

⚙ Work in groups and act out the conversation.

⚙ Activity
Discussion: What do you think of the landlady?

## Vocabulary extension

| | | | | | | |
|---|---|---|---|---|---|---|
| 负责 | fùzé | be responsible for | | 热情 | rèqíng | warm, enthusiastic |
| 小气 | xiǎoqi | stingy | | 大方 | dàfang | generous |
| 同屋 | tóngwū | roommate | | 室友 | shìyǒu | roommate |
| 吵架 | chǎojià | to quarrel, to argue | | | | |
| 岂有此理 | qǐyǒucǐlǐ | outrageous | | | | |

_____     _____

_____     _____

## Text

(Wang Ying and Zhang Yuanyuan have just moved into the apartment they are renting. They never thought that there would be something wrong with the air-conditioner so soon.)

Zhāng Yuányuan: Zhème rè de tiān, fángjiān li méiyǒu kōngtiáo, zhēn ràng rén shēngqì!

张　园园：这么热的天，房间里没有空调，真让人生气！ `complaint`

Wáng Yīng: Shì a, tài búxiànghuà le! Gěi fángdōng dǎ ge diànhuà, kàn tā zěnme huídá.

王　英：是啊，太不像话了！给房东打个电话，看她怎么回答。(dials the telephone) `complaint`

Shì Qián tàitai ma?

是钱太太吗？

Qián Tàitai: Shì wǒ. Shénme shìr?

钱太太：是我。什么事儿？

Wáng Yīng: Kōngtiáo yǐjīng chāi xiàlai hǎo jǐ tiān le, xiūhǎo le méiyǒu a?

王　英：空调已经拆下来好几天了，修好了没有啊？

Qián Tàitai: Duìbuqǐ, hái méi xiūhǎo. Shīfu shuō, zhè tái kōngtiáo tài jiù le, méi bànfǎ xiū.

钱太太：对不起，还没修好。师傅说，这台空调太旧了，没办法修。

Wáng Yīng: Nà zěnme bàn?

王　英：那怎么办？

Qián Tàitai: Zhège …

钱太太：这个……

Zhāng Yuányuan: Nín jiù náchū yìdiǎnr qián lái mǎi yì tái xīn de ma!

张　园园：您就拿出一点儿钱来买一台新的嘛！

Qián Tàitai:　Kànlái zhǐhǎo huàn tái xīn de.
(takes the telephone) 钱太太：看来只好 换台新的。

Zhāng Yuányuan:　Nà jiù máfan nín kuàidiǎnr mǎilái zhuāng shàngqù.
张　园园：那就麻烦您快点儿买来 装 上去。

Qián Tàitai:　Wǒ yì yǒu kòng jiù qù mǎi.
钱太太：我一有空 就去买。

Zhāng Yuányuan:　Nín shénme shíhou yǒu kòng ne?　Wǒmen rèsǐ le!
张　园园：您 什么时候有 空 呢? 我们热死了!

complaint

hesitation

Qián Tàitai:　Zhège　…　zhēn bù hǎo yìsi.　Zhèyàng ba,
钱太太：这个……真不好意思。这样吧,

apology

wǒ jīntiān xiàwǔ jiù qù diànqì shāngdiàn kàn yíxià.　Rúguǒ néng mǎidào
我今天下午就去电器 商店 看一下。如果 能 买到

dehua,　mǎshàng jiù ràng shāngdiàn sòng guòlai.
的话，马上 就 让 商店 送过来。

## ⬇ 注释　Zhùshì　Notes

（一）好几天

quite a few days

（二）不好意思

"How embarrassing!" Here it just means "sorry."

Unit
9

# 9.3 Language Points

❋ V. + Directional Complement

The direction verb immdiately following the verb and indicating the direction of the action is called the directional complement; for example:

（1）他从商店<u>买来</u>一台空调。

（2）这合同我们可以<u>带回去</u>吗?

If the verb has an object of place, the object should follow 进, 出, 上, 下 … but precede 来 or 去; for example:

（1）他<u>走进</u>房间。

（2）他<u>走进</u>房间<u>来</u>了。

（3）我们得<u>走上</u>楼<u>去</u>。

If the object is a thing, it may have three possible positions:

（1）他<u>带</u>了一份合同<u>回来</u>。

（2）他<u>带回</u>一份合同<u>来</u>。

（3）他<u>带回来</u>一份合同。

⚙ Comeplete the following sentences using V. + directional complement.

（1）我住在六楼，没有电梯，每天走_____走_____，特别累。

（2）我们一走_____饭店，服务员就走_____，请我们坐_____，问我们想来点儿什么。

（3）他正在房间里坐着，一看见我，就马上站_____，从包里拿_____一份合同，让我签字。

（4）昨天我去看我父母亲，给他们带____了一些食品，可是他们不喜欢，结果，我又带____了。

⬇ 文化点　Wénhuàdiǎn　**Cultural notes**

Due to China's large population housing in the cities was inadequate for a long time. Previously, a welfare-housing allocation system (fúlì fēnfáng zhìdù) was in use, whereby organizations would provide their employees with housing in return for a minimal amount of rent. Things are different now; employees' income has been increased greatly, and the welfare-housing allocation system has been abandoned. Now, employees usually have to purchase their own residences. Since the beginning of the economic reform, many commercial high-rise apartment buildings have been built, so the housing situation has improved considerably.

However, in the recent decades, the housing price in China's mid-sized and big cities has begun to soar. Regular employees are under great pressure when purchasing their own home, which has become one of the hot issues of the modern day.

# Unit 10

## Wǒ Kǒngpà Tīng Bu Dǒng
## 我 恐怕 听 不 懂
## I'm Afraid I Don't Understand

### Learning objectives

❋ Expressing actions, behaviors and the potentiality of their result

❋ Talking about recreational activities

❋ Chinese dramas

### Key sentences

Wǒ kǒngpà tīng bu dǒng.
我 恐怕 听不懂。

I'm afraid I don't understand.

Piào mǎi de dào ma?
票 买 得 到 吗?

Can you buy the tickets?

Tā lèi de lián huà dōu shuō bu chūlai le.
她累得连话都 说不出来了。

She is too tired to even speak.

Kànlái, wǒ pá bu dào shāndǐng le.
看来,我爬不到 山顶 了。

It looks like I won't make it to the top of the mountain.

# 10.1

Piào Mǎi De Dào Ma?

## 票 买 得 到 吗?
## Can you get the tickets?

**Preliminary exercises**

① Warm up

你知道京剧吗？你觉得京剧怎么样？

你看过中国电影吗？能说出一位中国的电影演员的名字吗？

② Learn the following words and form correct sentences with the words under the teacher's guidance.

（1）好 他 眼睛 不，戴 得 眼镜

（2）出发 我们 早点儿 最好，迟到 别 了

（3）开 快 一点儿 得 请，赶 要 飞机 我

（4）上下班 时间 厉害 堵车 很 这里

（5）起床 看 报纸 他 早上 每天 一 就

（6）演员 有名 京剧 一位 非常 的 他 是

③ Fill in the blanks according to the recording.

（1）菜太多了，我们_____。

（2）黑板上的字太小，我看_____。

（3）明天的车票还_____？

（4）不堵车的话肯定_____，堵车的话，就_____了。

Question:

What special qualities do the added words have in terms of sentence structure?

③（1）菜太多了，我们吃不完。
（2）黑板上的字太小，我看不清楚。
（3）明天的车票还买得到吗？
（4）不堵车的话肯定来得及，堵车的话，就来不及了。

Listening script

**Words and expressions**

| | | | | |
|---|---|---|---|---|
| 1. | 场 | ( MW ) | chǎng | measure word for events like movies, operas, sports matches, or rain |
| 2. | 京剧 | ( N. ) | Jīngjù | Beijing Opera |
| 3. | 武打戏 | | wǔdǎxì | acrobatic fighting drama |
| | 武打 | ( N. ) | wǔdǎ | acrobatic fighting |
| | 戏 | ( N. ) | xì | drama, opera |
| 4. | 电影 | ( N. ) | diànyǐng | movie |
| 5. | 功夫片 | | gōngfupiàn | kung fu movie |
| | 功夫 | ( N. ) | gōngfu | kung fu (martial arts) |
| 6. | 演员 | ( N. ) | yǎnyuán | actor, actress |
| 7. | 有名 | ( Adj. ) | yǒumíng | famous |
| 8. | 座位 | ( N. ) | zuòwèi | seat |
| 9. | 眼睛 | ( N. ) | yǎnjing | eye |
| 10. | 报纸 | ( N. ) | bàozhǐ | newspaper |
| 11. | 杂志 | ( N. ) | zázhì | magazine |
| 12. | 懂 | ( V. ) | dǒng | understand |
| 13. | 出租车 | ( N. ) | chūzūchē | taxi |
| 14. | 堵车 | ( V.O. ) | dǔchē | traffic jam |
| 15. | 放心 | ( V.O.) | fàngxīn | don't worry |
| 16. | 出发 | ( V. ) | chūfā | set off |
| 17. | 赶 | ( V. ) | gǎn | rush for |
| 18. | 挺 | ( Adv. ) | tǐng | very |
| 19. | 最好 | ( Adv. ) | zuìhǎo | had better; it would be better |

⚙ Listen to the dialogue and answer the following questions in Chinese.

（1）今天晚上高一飞请王英干什么？

（2）王英有什么担心？高一飞为什么请她放心？

（3）京剧几点开始？他们几点出发？怎么去？

⚙ Listen to the recording while reading the text on the next page.

⚙ Read the text aloud and try not to look at the pinyin.

⚙ Work in groups and act out the conversation.

⚙ Activity

Students: Introduce a Chinese celebrity.

## Vocabulary extension

| | | | | | | |
|---|---|---|---|---|---|---|
| 戏剧 | xìjù | drama | 传统 | chuántǒng | tradition(al) |
| 水平 | shuǐpíng | level | 现代 | xiàndài | modern |
| 艺术 | yìshù | art | 体育 | tǐyù | sports |
| 明星 | míngxīng | star, famous performer or athlete | 粉丝 | fěnsī | fans |
| 表演 | biǎoyǎn | performance; to perform | 精彩 | jīngcǎi | wonderful |

Unit
10

## Text

(Gao Yifei invites Wang Ying to watch a Beijing Opera.)

Gāo Yīfēi: Jīntiān wǎnshang yǒu yì chǎng jīngjù, zánmen yìqǐ qù kàn ba,
高一飞：今天 晚上 有一场 京剧，咱们一起 去看吧，

zěnmeyàng?
怎么样？

Wáng Yīng: Wǒ kǒngpà tīng bu dǒng ba.
王 英：我恐怕 听不懂 吧。 worry

Gāo Yīfēi: Méi guānxi, shì wǔdǎxì, nǐ tīng bu dǒng, yídìng kàn de dǒng.
高一飞：没关系，是武打戏，你听不懂，一定看得懂。 reassurance

Wáng Yīng: Yǎnyuán yǒumíng ma?
王 英：演员有名 吗？

Gāo Yīfēi: Wǒ shuō bu chū tāmen de míngzi, búguò bàozhǐ shang shuō, nàxiē
高一飞：我说不出他们的名字，不过报纸上 说，那些

yǎnyuán dōu tǐng yǒumíng de.
演员都挺有名的。

Wáng Yīng: Piào mǎi de dào ma?
王 英：票买得到吗？

Gāo Yīfēi: Méi wèntí, kěndìng mǎi de dào.
高一飞：没问题，肯定买得到。

Wáng Yīng: Zuìhǎo shì qiánmiàn de zuòwèi. Wǒ yǎnjing bù hǎo, zuòzài
王 英：最好是 前面 的座位。我眼睛 不好， 坐在

128 ▶▶

hòumiàn　kàn bu qīngchu.
后面　看不清楚。

Gāo Yīfēi:　Nǐ fàngxīn ba.
高一飞：你放心吧。 `reassurance`

Wáng Yīng:　Nà hǎo,　zánmen jǐ diǎn chūfā?
王　英：那好，咱们几点出发？

Gāo Yīfēi:　Jīngjù wǎnshang qī diǎn kāishǐ,　zánmen liù diǎn yí kè　chūfā ba.
高一飞：京剧 晚上 七点开始，咱们 六点一刻 出发吧。

Wáng Yīng:　Bàn gè xiǎoshí gǎn de dào ma?
王　英：半个小时赶得到吗？

Gāo Yīfēi:　Gǎn de dào.　Zánmen zuò chūzūchē qù,　bù dǔchē　dehuà,
高一飞：赶得到。咱们坐出租车去，不堵车的话，

yí　kèzhōng jiù dào le.
一刻钟 就到了。

## 10.2

Lián Huà Dōu Shuō Bu Chūlai  Le

# 连话 都 说 不 出来 了

## Too tired to even speak

> **Preliminary exercises**

1 **Warm up**

你平时运动吗？你喜欢什么运动？

中国人一般喜欢什么运动？

2 **Learn the following words and form correct sentences with the words under the teacher's guidance.**

（1）要 多长时间 还 山顶 爬 到

（2）建议 跑步 出去 晚上 每天 你 我

（3）想 休息 安安静静 一会儿 我 地

（4）忙 平时 太，运动 没有 时间

（5）教 打 太极拳 你 我 吧

（6）忙 你 太 了，要 注意 身体 啊

3 **Fill in the blanks according to the recording.**

（1）词典太大，包太小，＿＿＿＿＿＿＿＿＿＿。

（2）我没买到票，今年春节我＿＿＿＿＿＿＿＿了。

（3）这么高的山，我们怎么＿＿＿＿＿＿＿＿啊！

（4）她气得连话都＿＿＿＿＿＿＿＿了。

Question:

What special qualities do the added words have in terms of sentence structure?

Listening script

3（1）词典太大，包太小，放不进去了。

（2）票没有买到，今年春节我回不去了。

（3）这么高的山，我们怎么爬得上去啊！

（4）她气得连话都说不出来了。

## Words and expressions

| | | | | |
|---|---|---|---|---|
| 1. | 平时 | ( TW ) | píngshí | (in) normal times; (at) ordinary times; ordinarily |
| 2. | 运动 | ( N. ) | yùndòng | physical exercise |
| 3. | 爬 | ( V. ) | pá | climb, crawl |
| 4. | 山顶 | ( N. ) | shāndǐng | mountaintop |
| 5. | 跑步 | | pǎobù | run, jog |
| | 跑 | ( V. ) | pǎo | run |
| 6. | 太极拳 | ( N. ) | tàijíquán | Taiji Boxing |
| 7. | 教 | ( V. ) | jiāo | teach |
| 8. | 建议 | ( V. & N. ) | jiànyì | suggest; suggestion |
| 9. | 注意 | ( V. ) | zhùyì | pay attention to |
| 10. | 动 | ( V. ) | dòng | move |
| 11. | 安静 | ( Adj. ) | ānjìng | quiet |
| 12. | 懒 | ( Adj. ) | lǎn | lazy |
| 13. | 话 | ( N. ) | huà | speech |
| 14. | 水 | ( N. ) | shuǐ | water |
| 15. | 连……都 / 也…… | | lián … dōu / yě … | even |
| 16. | 才 | ( Adv. ) | cái | only |
| 17. | 地 | ( Part. ) | de | used with an adverb or adverbial phrase to modify an action |

Unit 10

⚙ Listen to the dialogue and answer the following questions in Chinese.

（1）他们在干什么？

（2）李小雨怎么啦？

（3）田中、高一飞、王英对李小雨有什么建议？

⚙ Listen to the recording while reading the text on the next page.

⚙ Read the text aloud and try not to look at the pinyin.

⚙ Work in groups and act out the conversation.

⚙ Activity

Students: What sports do you like? What sugguestions do you have for your classmates?

## Vocabulary extension

| | | | | | | |
|---|---|---|---|---|---|---|
| 打篮球 | dǎ lánqiú | play basketball | | 打网球 | dǎ wǎngqiú | play tennis |
| 踢足球 | tī zúqiú | play football | | 下棋 | xiàqí | play chess |
| 辛苦 | xīnkǔ | laborious | | 同意 | tóngyì | to agree |
| 坚持 | jiānchí | persist in; stick to | | 放弃 | fàngqì | give up |

_____    _____

_____    _____

(On the weekend Gao Yifei, Martin, Wang Ying, Tanaka and Li Xiaoyu etc. are climbing mountain together in the countryside.)

Lǐ Xiǎoyǔ: Wǒ··· bù··· bù xíng le.
李 小 雨：我……不……不行了。

Tiánzhōng: Kàn, Xiǎoyǔ lèi de lián huà dōu shuō bu chūlai le.
田 中：看，小雨累得连话都说不出来了。

Gāo Yīfēi: Xiǎoyǔ pá bu dòng le, zánmen xiūxi xiūxi ba.
高一飞：小雨爬不动了，咱们休息休息吧。 suggestion

Lǐ Xiǎoyǔ: Ràng wǒ hē diǎnr shuǐ. ··· Dào shāndǐng hái yǒu duōshao lù?
李 小 雨：让我喝点儿水。……到山顶还有多少路？

Xiǎo Zhāng: Zánmen cái pále yíbàn, hái yǒu yíbàn.
王 英：咱们才爬了一半，还有一半。

Lǐ Xiǎoyǔ: Kànlái, wǒ pá bu dào shāndǐng le. Nǐmen shàng ba, wǒ zài shānxià
李 小 雨：看来，我爬不到山顶了。你们上吧，我在山下

děng nǐmen.
等你们。

Mǎdīng: Nǐ ya, píngshí yùndòng de tài shǎo.
马 丁：你呀，平时运动得太少。 correcting

Lǐ Xiǎoyǔ: Bú shì yùndòng de tài shǎo, shì shìr tài duō, duō de zuò bu wán, nǎ
李 小 雨：不是运动得太少，是事儿太多，多得做不完，哪

yǒu shíjiān yùndòng?
有时间运动？

Mǎdīng: Bú shì méiyǒu shíjiān, shì tài lǎn le ba?
马 丁：不是没有时间，是太懒了吧？

Wáng Yīng: Bù néng zhǐ xiǎngzhe gōngzuò, yě yào zhùyì xiūxi.
王 英：不能只想着工作，也要注意休息。 *giving advice*

Tiánzhōng: Wǒ jiànyì nǐ yǐhòu měi tiān zǎoshang chūqù pǎobù.
田 中：我建议你以后每天 早上 出去跑步。 *suggestion*

Gāo Yīfēi: Yǐhòu wǒ jiāo nǐ dǎ tàijíquán.
高一飞：以后我教你打太极拳。

Lǐ Xiǎoyǔ: Nǐmen kuài zǒu ba, ràng wǒ zài zhèr ān'ānjìngjìng de xiūxi
李小雨：你们 快走吧，让我在这儿安安静静地休息

yíhuìr.
一会儿。

 注释 Zhùshì **Notes**

（一）连话都说不出来

One can also say: "连话也说不出来." 连 … 都 / 也 … is a pattern for emphasis. Other examples: 这个问题太容易了，连孩子也能回答。/ 他太忙了，连饭都没有时间吃。

（二）小雨爬不动了

Here "V. + 得 / 不 + 动" means "to have or not have strength to do something." Another example: 我走不动了，休息休息吧。

（三）安安静静地休息一会儿

地 should be read "de" here. When disyllabic adjectives and the reduplicated forms of adjectives are used as adverbials to modify a verb, 地 should be used; for example: 她非常高兴地唱了一个歌。/ 她高高兴兴地唱了一个歌。

# 10.3　Language Points

### I. V. + 得/不 + Potential Complement

The inner elements of the V.-Comple. pattern, when it consists of the verb and the resultative complement, or the verb and the directional complement, are inseparable. But 得 / 不 can be inserted in most of these to indicate potentiality. "V. 得 Comple." means "can" and "V. 不 Comple." means "cannot."

E.g.（1）他说的话我都听得懂，你说的话我都听不懂。
（2）字写得太小，我们看不清楚。
（3）门太小了，汽车开不进去。

The interrogative pattern is "… 吗 ," or "V. 得 Comple. V. 不 Comple." For example:
（1）京剧票买得到吗?
（2）这本书一年学得完学不完?

When indicating permission or agreement, 能 or 可以 should be used instead of the "V. 得 / 不 Comple." pattern.

E.g. 对不起，你没买票，不能进去。

### II. A Summary of the Complements

Besides objects, various kinds of complements may follow the verb, to describe or comment on the action. Sometimes, the complement may follow the adjective to further explain the state or the degree.

**1. V. + Resultative Complement:**
（1）票卖完了。
（2）眼镜摔破了。
（3）他没说清楚。

**2. V. + Directional Complement:**
（1）他给我带来几块巧克力。
（2）我给他带去一盒茶叶。
（3）这台电视机是从他房间里搬出来的。

The elements of both "V. + Resultative Complement" and "V. + Directional Complement" are inseparable, almost like a word.

**3. V. + 得 / 不 + Potential Complement:**
（1）票买得到吗?
（2）我的汉语不太好，说不清楚。

Unit
10

135

（3）门关着，我们进不去。

（4）门太小，电视机太大，搬不出来。

This pattern is formed by inserting "得/不" into the structure of "V. + Resultative Complement" or "V. + Directional Complement."

### 4. V. + Predicative Complement:

（1）他打球打得不错。

（2）他球打得不错。

（3）他的汉语说得很好。

（4）他太忙了，忙得没有时间吃饭。

In this pattern, 得 must precede the complement. In fact, the complement is comments on the preceding verb or adjective.

### 5. V. + Complement of Quantity:

（1）今天比昨天冷一点儿。

（2）他吃饭吃了一个小时。

（3）这本书他已经看了两遍了。

The complement of quantity mainly indicates the distance, duration, or times/frequency of actions.

### 6. V. + Complement of Degree:

（1）工作了一天，我累极了。

（2）工作了一天，我累死了。

○ Complete the following sentences.

（1）我才学了半年汉语，中国的电影、电视我还_____。

（2）我平时运动太少，只能跑五千米，一万米我恐怕_____。

（3）你能帮我买一张中文的中国地图吗？在我们这里的大学书店里_____。

（4）门太小，这么大的汽车，肯定开_____，就让车停在门外吧。

（5）他心里有很多话，可是说_____，因为不知道该怎么说。

 文化点　Wénhuàdiǎn　**Cultural notes**

Dramatic opera, xìqǔ, is the traditional form of Chinese drama performed on stage. It includes Kunqu Opera (kūnqǔ), Beijing Opera (jīngjù), and many other regional and local opera forms. There are regional operas such as Shaoxing Opera (yuèjù), Cantonese Opera (yuèjù), Henan Opera (yùjù), Sichuan Opera (chuānjù), and Anhui Opera (huángméixì). In the Northeast, there are the Yangge Opera (yāngger), the song-and-dance duet (èrrénzhuàn), and other forms. Through over one hundred years of development, Beijing Opera has evolved a special artistic style and complex performance conventions. It enjoys popularity all over the country and has had great influence upon other forms of dramatic operas.

# Unit 11

## Wǒ Bǎ Qiánbāo Wàng Zài Chē Shang Le
## 我 把 钱包 忘 在 车 上 了
### I've Left My Wallet in the Car

### Learning objectives

* Expressing disposition of objects
* Expressing reproach and gratitude
* Narrating the process of an event

### Key sentences

Fù qián yǐhòu, nǐ bǎ qiánbāo fàng zài nǎr le?
付 钱 以后，你 把 钱包 放 在 哪儿了?
Where did you put your wallet after paying?

Wǒ bǎ tā rēng dào lājīxiāng li qù le.
我 把 它 扔 到 垃圾箱 里 去了。
I threw it into the garbage can.

Nǐ bǎ zhè wǔbǎi Měiyuán sòng gěi sījī le.
你 把 这 五百 美元 送 给 司机了。
You gave the five hundred US dollars to the driver.

Wǒ mǎshàng bǎ qiánbāo gěi nǐmen sòng guòlai.
我 马上 把 钱包 给 你们 送 过来。
I'll send the wallet over to you immediately.

# 11.1

Nǐ Bǎ Qiánbāo Fàng Zài Nǎr Le?

## 你把钱包 放在哪儿了?

## Where did you put your wallet?

**Preliminary exercises**

1 Warm up

你丢过东西吗? 后来找到了吗?

2 Learn the following words and form correct sentences with the words under the teacher's guidance.

（1）去 哪儿 你 刚才 了

（2）扔 一 个 球 过来 他 我 向

（3）放 在 你 的 钱包 左边 的 口袋 里 不是 吗

（4）放 在 不同 的 垃圾 不同 的 垃圾箱 里 应该

（5）回 家 赶快 你 吧，等 你 妈 你 在 呢

（6）你 怎么 搞 的! 不记得 生词 上个 星期 学 的 都 了?

3 Fill in the blanks according to the recording.

（1）我把电脑放_____了。

（2）我把钱包忘_____了。

（3）我把公寓租_____了。

（4）我把发票扔_____了。

Question:

What similarities do the above sentences have in terms of sentence structure?

## Words and expressions

| | | | | |
|---|---|---|---|---|
| 1. | 钱包 | ( N. ) | qiánbāo | wallet, purse |
| 2. | 美元 | ( N. ) | měiyuán | US dollar |
| 3. | 口袋 | ( N. ) | kǒudài | pocket |
| 4. | 司机 | ( N. ) | sījī | driver |
| 5. | 发票 | ( N. ) | fāpiào | receipt |
| 6. | 垃圾箱 | | lājīxiāng | garbage can |
| | 垃圾 | ( N. ) | lājī | garbage |
| 7. | 放 | ( V. ) | fàng | put, place |
| 8. | 丢 | ( V. ) | diū | lose |
| 9. | 扔 | ( V. ) | rēng | throw |
| 10. | 搞 | ( V. ) | gǎo | do |
| 11. | 记得 | ( V. ) | jìde | remember |
| 12. | 记住 | | jìzhù | memorize |
| 13. | 觉得 | ( V. ) | juéde | feel, think |
| 14. | 刚才 | ( TW ) | gāngcái | just now |
| 15. | 没用 | ( Adj. ) | méiyòng | useless |
| 16. | 糟糕 | ( Adj. ) | zāogāo | too bad; how terrible |
| 17. | 赶快 | ( Adv. ) | gǎnkuài | quickly; at once |
| 18. | 把 | ( Prep. ) | bǎ | used to advance the object of a verb to the position before it |

Unit
11

⚙ Listen to the dialogue and answer the following questions in Chinese.

（1）发生了什么糟糕的事？

（2）马丁的钱包里有多少钱？

（3）马丁还记得那辆出租车的车号吗？

⚙ Listen to the recording while reading the text on the next page.

⚙ Read the text aloud and try not to look at the pinyin.

⚙ Work in groups and act out the conversation.

⚙ Activity

Discussion: Do you think the cab driver will return the wallet to Martin?

## Vocabulary extension

| | | | | | | |
|---|---|---|---|---|---|---|
| 保存 | bǎocún | to keep | | 粗心 | cūxīn | careless |
| 心疼 | xīnténg | feel sorry | | 发现 | fāxiàn | to discover |
| 乘客 | chéngkè | passenger | | 联系 | liánxì | to contact |
| 贪心 | tānxīn | greedy | | 热心 | rèxīn | warm-hearted |

## Text

(After touring the city, Martin and his parents go to the hotel.)

Mǎdīng: Āiyā, wǒ de qiánbāo ne?
马 丁：哎呀，我的钱包呢？

Mǔqīn: Shì bu shì diū le?
母 亲：是不是丢了？

Mǎdīng: Bù kěnéng ya, gāngcái xià chē de shíhou, shì wǒ fù de qián, nà
马 丁：不可能呀，刚才下车的时候，是我付的钱，那

shíhou qiánbāo hái zài.
时候钱包还在。

Mǔqīn: Fù qián yǐhòu, nǐ bǎ qiánbāo fàng zài nǎr le?
母 亲：付钱以后，你把钱包放在哪儿了？

Mǎdīng: Zāogāo! Wǒ bǎ qiánbāo wàng zài zuòwèi shang le.
马 丁：糟糕！我把钱包忘在座位上了。

Fùqīn: Nǐ zěnme gǎo de!
父 亲：你怎么搞的！ reproach

Mǔqīn: Xiànzài zěnme bàn?
母 亲：现在怎么办？

Fùqīn: Gǎnkuài gěi chūzūchē gōngsī dǎ diànhuà. Nǐ hái jìde chēhào ma?
父 亲：赶快给出租车公司打电话。你还记得车号吗？

Mǎdīng: Wǒ yìdiǎnr yě xiǎng bu qǐlai le.
马 丁：我一点儿也想不起来了。 remembering

Fùqīn: Fāpiào ná le ma?
父 亲：发票拿了吗？

马 丁： Wǒ juéde fāpiào méiyòng, jiù bǎ tā rēng dào lājīxiāng li qù le.
马 丁：我觉得发票没用，就把它扔到垃圾箱里去了。

母 亲： Qiánbāo li yǒu duōshao qián?
母 亲：钱包里有多少钱？

马 丁： Dàgài wǔbǎi měiyuán.
马 丁：大概五百美元。

母 亲： Nǐ bǎ zhè wǔbǎi měiyuán sòng gěi sījī le.
母 亲：你把这五百美元送给司机了。

## 注释 Zhùshì Notes

（一）我的钱包呢？

"Noun phrase + 呢" used at the beginning of a dialogue means … 在哪儿.

（二）是我付的钱

This sentence is a 是 … 的 structure. Here the doer 我 is emphasized. In the sentence pattern 是 … 的, if the verb has an object, the object is often placed after 的.

（三）怎么搞的

怎么搞的 bears a tone of resentment or blame.

（四）想不起来

想不起来 means "can't remember."

# 11.2

Wǒ Mǎshàng Bǎ Qiánbāo Gěi Nǐmen Sòng Guòlai
## 我 马上 把 钱包 给 你们 送 过来

### I'll bring the wallet over to you immediately

## Preliminary exercises

1 Warm up

如果你在国外旅行，可是你把护照丢了，你该怎么办?

2 Learn the following words and form correct sentences with the words under the teacher's guidance.

（1）是 孩子 一 个 诚实 真 的 这

（2）打 电话 给 宾馆 总台 你 可以

（3）护照 你 有 没有 其他 证件 或者

（4）发 给 我 宾馆 的 地址 把 请

（5）交 给 老师 作业 记住 一定 要 明天 把

（6）有 地址 电话号码 我 的 名片 上 和

3 Fill in the blanks according to the recording.

（1）我马上把东西给你们送_____。

（2）我们把包里的东西拿_____看看吧。

（3）你怎么把空调拆_____了?

（4）我们不可以把这些东西拿_____。

Question:

What similarities do the above sentences have in terms of sentence structure?

Listening script

③（1）我马上把东西给你们送过来。
（2）我们把包里的东西拿出来看看吧。
（3）你怎么把空调拆下来了?
（4）我们不可以把这些东西拿回家去。

**Words and expressions**

| 1. | 证件 | ( N. ) | zhèngjiàn | document |
| 2. | 护照 | ( N. ) | hùzhào | passport |
| 3. | 宾馆 | ( N. ) | bīnguǎn | guesthouse, hotel |
| 4. | 总台 | ( N. ) | zǒngtái | front desk; operator |
| 5. | 纸 | ( N. ) | zhǐ | paper |
| 6. | 卡片 | ( N. ) | kǎpiàn | card |
| 7. | 名片 | ( N. ) | míngpiàn | name card; visiting card |
| 8. | 地址 | ( N. ) | dìzhǐ | address |
| 9. | 乘客 | ( N. ) | chéngkè | passenger |
| 10. | 发现 | ( V. ) | fāxiàn | discover, find |
| 11. | 感谢 | ( V. ) | gǎnxiè | thank |
| 12. | 其他 | ( Pron. ) | qítā | other |
| 13. | 它 | ( Pron. ) | tā | it |
| 14. | 交 | ( V. ) | jiāo | hand in; give |
| 15. | 转 | ( V. ) | zhuǎn | transfer |
| 16. | 骂 | ( V. ) | mà | scold |
| 17. | 诚实 | ( Adj. ) | chéngshí | honest |
| 18. | 顿 | ( MW ) | dùn | measure word for meals, scolding, etc |

⚙ Listen to the dialogue and answer the following questions in Chinese.
  （1）司机为什么给马丁打电话？
  （2）司机是怎么知道马丁的电话的？

⚙ Listen to the recording while reading the text on the next page.

⚙ Read the text aloud and try not to look at the pinyin.

⚙ Work in groups and act out the conversation.

⚙ Activity
Perform a skit demonstrating the conversation between the cab driver and the passenger after the passenger saw the wallet.

## Vocabulary extension

| | | | | | | |
|---|---|---|---|---|---|---|
| 客人 | kèren | guest | 奇怪 | qíguài | strange |
| 行李 | xíngli | luggage | 信用卡 | xìnyòngkǎ | credit card |
| 捡 | jiǎn | pick up | 小费 | xiǎofèi | tip |
| 责怪 | zéguài | to blame | 表扬 | biǎoyáng | to praise |

Unit
**11**

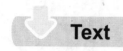 

(The telephone rings as Martin is feeling thoroughly frustrated.)

Mǎdīng: Wèi, nǎ wèi?
马 丁：喂，哪位？

Sījī: Wǒ shì chūzū qìchē sījī, jīntiān shàngwǔ nǐmen zuòguo wǒ de chē.
司 机：我是出租汽车司机，今天上午你们坐过我的车。

Nǐmen shì bu shì bǎ shénme dōngxi wàng zài chē shang le?
你们是不是把什么东西忘在车上了？

Mǎdīng: Duìduìduì, Wǒmen bǎ qiánbāo wàng zài chē shang le.
马 丁：对对对，我们把钱包忘在车上了。

Sījī: Wǒ mǎshàng bǎ qiánbāo gěi nǐmen sòng guòlai.
司 机：我马上把钱包给你们送过来。

Mǎdīng: Āiyā, tài gǎnxiè nín le! Nín shì zěnme fāxiàn wǒmen de
马 丁：哎呀，太感谢您了！您是怎么发现我们的

qiánbāo de?
钱包的？ [curiosity]

Sījī: Yǒu yí wèi chéngkè kàndàole qiánbāo, bǎ tā jiāo gěile wǒ.
司 机：有一位乘客看到了钱包，把它交给了我。

Mǎdīng: Zhēn shì yí wèi hǎorén, Nà nín zěnme huì zhīdào wǒmen de diànhuà
马 丁：真是一位好人。那您怎么会知道我们的电话

hàomǎ ne?
号码呢？ [curiosity]

Sījī: Wǒmen bǎ qiánbāo li de dōngxi ná chūlai yí kàn, fāxiàn lǐmiàn yǒu
司 机：我们把钱包里的东西拿出来一看，发现里面有

yì zhāng zhǐ,　shàngmiàn yǒu nǐmen zhù de bīnguǎn de míngzi hé

一 张 纸，上面 有你们住的宾馆的名字和

dìzhǐ.　Wǒ dǎ diànhuà gěi bīnguǎn,　zǒngtái jiù bǎ diànhuà zhuǎn

地址。我打电话 给宾馆，总台就把电话 转

dàole　nǐmen fángjiān.

到了你们房间。

Mǎdīng:　Zhēn shì tài máfan nín le.

马　丁：真 是太麻烦您了。

Sījī:　Méi shénme.　Nǐmen yídìng hěn zháojí ba?

司　机：没 什么。你们一定很着急吧？

Mǎdīng:　Kěbushì.　Gāngcái wǒ mā hái bǎ wǒ màle　yí dùn ne.

马　丁：可不是。刚才我妈还把我骂了一顿呢。

Qiánbāo li yǒu hùzhào hé　qítā zhèngjiàn,　yàoshi diū le

钱包 里有护照和其他证件，要是丢了

jiù máfan le.

就麻烦了。

## 注释　Zhùshì　Notes

（一）可不是

　　可不是 means "yes," "of course."

（二）要是丢了就麻烦了

　　要是 / 如果 and 就 are often used together. Other examples: 你要是没有时间，就别去了。/ 如果你不方便的话，我就不去了。

# 11.3  Language Points

❀ The 把 ba Sentence

A sentence with 把 … as an adverbial is called the 把 (ba) sentence. This sentence pattern indicates that somebody does something to a definite object and the object is usually effected or changed to a certain extent.

The sentence pattern with 把 is as follows:

> ## S. + 把 O. definite + V + other elements

E.g. （1）妈妈刚才把我骂了一顿。
　　（2）我马上把钱包给你们送过来。
　　（3）你把这五百美元送给司机了。

When the verb is followed by 在 …/ 给 …/ 到 …, the 把 sentence pattern must be used to introduce the object.

> ## 把 + O.definite + V. 在 / 给 / 到 …

E.g. （1）他把花儿放在桌子上。
　　（2）他把花儿送给他女朋友。
　　（3）他把花儿送到女朋友家里。

When the verb is followed by a disyllabic directional complement and a place expression, the 把 sentence pattern must be used to introduce the object.

> ## 把 +O. definite + V.+ Directional Comple. + place + Directional Comple.

E.g. （1）我们把这些东西搬上楼去吧。
　　（2）你不能把这些钱拿回家去。

**Notice:**

（1）When the verb does not denote domination or influence, the 把 sentence is not normally used. So we do not say, 我把他知道, or 我把他见了面.

（2）The object of 把 is definite, so instead of saying 我把一本词典买来了, we should say 我把词典

买来了 / 我把那本词典买来了.

（3）Time expressions, optative verbs, or negative words should precede 把. E.g. 我昨天把那本书还给图书馆了。/ 我不想把那本书还给图书馆。/ 我还没有把那本书还给图书馆。

 Complete the following sentences.

（1）我已经把洗衣机_____。

（2）请你赶快把你的航班号_____。

（3）我们已经把你的参观活动都_____。

（4）你能不能把那张新地图_____。

（5）明天请你把合同_____。

## 文化点　Wénhuàdiǎn　Cultural notes

A "hotel" is usually called "bīnguǎn" in Chinese. However, "xxx (dà) fàndiàn" or "xxx (dà) jiǔjiā" may also be used. The words "fàndiàn" can mean restaurant or hotel; a restaurant is called a "fànguǎnr" in the north. Similarly, "xx jiǔjiā" could also denote a restaurant or a hotel. Some organizations, factories, and schools may provide inexpensive and simply furnished guesthouses for their guests or visitors. These are called "zhāodàisuǒ."

\*　　　\*　　　\*

When you visit China, you may want to remember the following handy telephone numbers:

120: jiùhù, for emergency, rescue

119: huǒjǐng, to report a fire

110: bàojǐng, to report a burglary

Unit
11

149

# Unit 12

## Chàdiǎnr Bèi Qìchē Zhuàngle Yíxià
## 差点儿 被 汽车 撞 了一下
## I Was Nearly Hit by a Car

### Learning objectives

❋ Expressing unhappy experiences

❋ Expressing sympathy, condolences and regrets

❋ Narrating an unhappy incident

### Key sentences

Wǒ chàdiánr bèi qìchē zhuàngle.
我 差点儿 被 汽车 撞 了。

I was nearly hit by a car.

Zìxíngchē jiào rén jièzǒu le.
自行车 叫 人 借走 了。

Somebody borrowed the bicycle.

Hé li de yú dōu bèi dúsǐ le.
河里的 鱼 都 被毒死了。

All the fish in the river were killed by poison.

Lù liǎngbiān de shù dōu bèi kǎndǎo le.
路 两边 的 树 都 被 砍 倒 了。

All the trees on both sides of the road were cut down.

# 12.1

Zìxíngchē Diū Le

## 自行车 丢了

# The bicycle was missing

**Preliminary exercises**

1️⃣ Warm up

你的电脑中过病毒吗？

你的东西丢过吗？

2️⃣ Learn the following words and form correct sentences with the words under the teacher's guidance.

（1）倒霉 你 真 够 的

（2）对不起， 丢 我 文件 把 了

（3）坏 透 运气 我 今天 了

（4）中 病毒 我 的 电脑 了

（5）要 小心 马路 过 的时候

（6）装 杀毒 软件 电脑 这 台 没 还

3️⃣ Fill in the blanks according to the recording.

（1）眼镜____他摔破了。

（2）我的词典____小雨拿走了。

（3）他的自行车____人借去了。

（4）他刚才差点儿____汽车撞了。

Question:

In the above sentences, what do 被, 叫 and 让 mean?

Unit 12

# Words and expressions

| | | | | |
|---|---|---|---|---|
| 1. | 红绿灯 | ( N. ) | hónglùdēng | traffic lights |
| | 灯 | ( N. ) | dēng | lamp, light |
| 2. | 电脑 | ( N. ) | diànnǎo | computer |
| 3. | 软件 | ( N. ) | ruǎnjiàn | software |
| 4. | 硬件 | ( N. ) | yìngjiàn | hardware |
| 5. | 文件 | ( N. ) | wénjiàn | document |
| 6. | 中 | ( V. ) | zhòng | be affected by; be hit by |
| 7. | 病毒 | ( N. ) | bìngdú | virus |
| | 毒 | ( V. &. N. &. Adj. ) | dú | (to) poison; virus, drugs; poisonous |
| 8. | 打开 | ( V. ) | dǎkāi | open |
| 9. | 杀毒 | ( V. O.) | shādú | kill the virus |
| | 杀 | ( V. ) | shā | kill |
| 10. | 帮忙 | ( V. O. ) | bāngmáng | lend a hand; do a favor |
| 11. | 运气 | ( N. ) | yùnqi | luck |
| 12. | 倒霉 | ( Adj. ) | dǎoméi | of bad luck |
| 13. | 小心 | ( Adj. ) | xiǎoxīn | careful |
| 14. | 够 | ( V. & Adv. ) | gòu | be enough; enough |
| 15. | 透 | ( Adj. & Adv. ) | tòu | thorough; fully |
| 16. | 差点儿 | ( Adv. ) | chàdiǎnr | nearly |
| 17. | 又 | ( Adv. ) | yòu | again |
| 18. | 被 | ( Prep. ) | bèi | by |

⚙ Listen to the dialogue and answer the following questions in Chinese.

（1）王英的电脑怎么了？

（2）王英的自行车是什么时候丢的？

⚙ Listen to the recording while reading the text on the next page.

⚙ Read the text aloud and try not to look at the pinyin.

⚙ Work in groups and act out the conversation.

⚙ Activity

Students: What bad experiences have occurred in your life?

## Vocabulary extension

| | | | | | | |
|---|---|---|---|---|---|---|
| 幸运 | xìngyùn | lucky | | 碰巧 | pèngqiǎo | by chance |
| 信息 | xìnxī | information | | 下载 | xiàzài | to download |

_____                    _____

_____                    _____

Unit
12

Wáng Yīng:　　Wǒ jīntiān　yùnqi　huàitòu le!
王　英：我今天运气坏透了！  dismay

Mǎdīng:　　Zěnme la?
马　丁：怎么啦？

Wáng Yīng:　　Zǎoshang qǐlái　yǐhòu,　　yì　dǎkāi diànnǎo,　　jiù　fāxiàn yǒu wèntí:
王　英：早上 起来以后，一打开电脑，就发现有问题：

wénjiàn zhǎo bu dào le!
文件 找不到了！

Mǎdīng:　　Diànnǎo huài le?
马　丁：电脑坏了？

Wáng Yīng:　　Yídìng　shì zhòng bìngdú le!
王　英：一定是 中 病毒了！

Mǎdīng:　　Nǐ méi zhuāng shādú ruǎnjiàn ma?
马　丁：你没 装 杀毒软件吗？

Wáng Yīng: Zhuāngle,　méiyòng.
王　英：装了，没用。

Mǎdīng:　　Bù kěnéng ba.　　Nà　nǐ　zěnmebàn ne?
马　丁：不可能吧。那你怎么办呢？

Wáng Yīng:　　Wǒ yǒu ge péngyou　kěyǐ bāngmáng. Wǒ qí zìxíngchē　qù tā jiā,　lùshang
王　英：我有个朋友可以帮忙。我骑自行车去他家，路上

qí de　tài kuài,　méi zhùyì hónglǜdēng,　chàdiǎnr　bèi qìchē zhuàngle.
骑得太快，没注意红绿灯，差点儿被汽车撞了。

Mǎdīng:　　Nǐ tài　zháojí le.
马　丁：你太着急了。

Wáng Yīng: Dàole tā jiā, dǎkāi yí kàn, wénjiàn yòu yǒu le! Tā shuō, kěnéng
王 英：到了他家，打开一看，文件又有了！他说，可能

shì yìngjiàn yǒu wèntí.
是硬件有问题。

Mǎdīng: Wénjiàn méi diū jiù hǎo.
马 丁：文件 没丢就好。

Wáng Yīng: Kěshì, cóng tā jiā chūlai, wǒ fāxiàn zìxíngchē bú jiàn le.
王 英：可是，从他家出来，我发现自行车不见了。

Mǎdīng: Zìxíngchē diū le?
马 丁：自行车丢了？

Wáng Yīng: Kěbushì.
王 英：可不是。

Mǎdīng: Nǐ zhēn gòu dǎoméi de.
马 丁：你真够倒霉的。 sympathy

## 注释 Zhùshì Notes

坏透了

... 透了 is an exclamatory sentence indicating a high degree.

# 12.2

Hé Li De Yú Dōu Bèi Dúsǐ Le
## 河里的鱼 都 被毒死了
## All the fish in the river were killed by poison

## Preliminary exercises

1. Warm up

   你觉得现在环境污染严重吗?

2. Learn the following words and form correct sentences with the words under the teacher's guidance.

   (1) 变 清 水 河 里 的 了
   (2) 保护 好 环境 一定 要 我们
   (3) 真 不错 味道 小吃 那儿 的
   (4) 卖 掉 他 老 房子 把 了, 真 可惜!
   (5) 规定 政府 砍 树 不 可以 随便
   (6) 严重 环境 污染 好像 越来越 了

3. Listen to the recording and write down sentences.

   (1) _____ 。
   (2) _____ 。
   (3) _____ 。
   (4) _____ 。

   Question:

   To which of the above sentences can 被 be added?

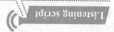

Listening script

[3] (1) 河里的鱼都被毒死了。
(2) 这条河的水越来越脏的。
(3) 那座旧房子马上就要拆掉了。
(4) 我每次都会在书架上了。

156

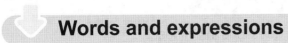

## Words and expressions

| | | | | |
|---|---|---|---|---|
| 1. | 变化 | ( N. ) | biànhuà | change |
| 2. | 政府 | ( N. ) | zhèngfǔ | government |
| 3. | 草地 | ( N. ) | cǎodì | lawn |
| 4. | 小吃 | ( N. ) | xiǎochī | snacks, refreshments |
| 5. | 味道 | ( N. ) | wèidao | taste |
| 6. | 污染 | ( N. & V. ) | wūrǎn | pollution; pollute |
| 7. | 严重 | ( Adj. ) | yánzhòng | serious |
| 8. | 随便 | ( Adj. ) | suíbiàn | casual, informal, random |
| 9. | 可惜 | ( Adj. ) | kěxī | pitiful; it's a pity |
| 10. | 清 | ( Adj. ) | qīng | clear |
| 11. | 栽 | ( V. ) | zāi | plant |
| 12. | 砍 | ( V. ) | kǎn | cut, chop |
| 13. | 变 | ( V. ) | biàn | change, become |
| 14. | 保护 | ( V. ) | bǎohù | protect |
| 15. | 相信 | ( V. ) | xiāngxìn | believe |
| 16. | 各种 | | gè zhǒng | all kinds of |
| 17. | 掉 | ( V. ) | diào | fall, drop |
| 18. | 好像 | ( Adv. ) | hǎoxiàng | as if; it seems … |

Unit
12

⚙ Listen to the dialogue and answer the following questions in Chinese.
（1）这条河几年前怎么样？现在呢？
（2）杰克怎么知道这些树都是新栽的？
（3）那些草地都是新的吗？那儿以前是什么？

⚙ Listen to the recording while reading the text on the next page.

⚙ Read the text aloud and try not to look at the pinyin.

⚙ Work in groups and act out the conversation.

⚙ Activity
Students: What measures should be taken to protect the environment?

## Vocabulary extension

| 街 | jiē | street | 湖 | hú | lake |
|---|---|---|---|---|---|
| 减少 | jiǎnshǎo | to decrease; decrease | 限制 | xiànzhì | to restrict; restriction |
| 建设 | jiànshè | to construct; construction | 法律 | fǎlù | law |
| 治理 | zhìlǐ | to administer; put in order | 改善 | gǎishàn | to improve |
| 发展 | fāzhǎn | to develop; development | | | |

_____ _____

_____ _____

(Xiao Huang accompanies Jack on a city tour. Jack has some memories of the city because he visited there several years ago.)

remembering

Jiékè: Wǒ jìde jǐ nián qián wǒ lái zhèr de shíhou, zhè tiáo hé wūrǎn
杰 克：我记得几年前我来这儿的时候，这条河污染

hěn yánzhòng. Hé li de yú dōu bèi dúsǐ le.
很 严重，河里的鱼都被毒死了。

Xiǎo Huáng: Xiànzài héshuǐ biànqīng le, nǐ kàn, hé li yòu yǒu yú le.
小 黄：现在河水变清了，你看，河里又有鱼了。

Jiékè: Biànhuà tài dà le！ Rúguǒ bù lái kànkan dehuà, zhēn nán xiāngxìn!
杰 克：变化太大了！如果不来看看的话，真难相信！

— Zhèxiē shù dōu shì yì-liǎng nián qián zāi de ba?
——这些树都是一两年前栽的吧？

Xiǎo Huáng: Shì a, Nǐ zěnme zhīdào?
小 黄：是啊。你怎么知道？

Jiékè: Shàng cì wǒ lái de shíhou, zhèr zhèngzài xiū lù, lù liǎngbiān de shù
杰 克：上次我来的时候，这儿正在修路，路两边的树

dōu bèi kǎndǎo le.
都被砍倒了。

Xiǎo Huáng: Xiànzài, zhèngfǔ guīdìng bù néng suíbiàn kǎn shù.
小 黄：现在，政府规定不能随便砍树。

Jiékè: Nà jǐ kuài cǎodì yě búcuò. — Yí, wǒ jìde nàr yǐqián
杰 克：那几块草地也不错。——咦，我记得那儿以前

hǎoxiàng shì  yìxiē  xiǎo fàndiàn,   mài gè zhǒng xiǎochī.
好像是一些小饭店，卖各种小吃。 remembering

Xiǎo Huáng:   Nàxiē  jiù  fángzi zǎo jiù chāidiào le.
小　黄：那些旧房子早就拆掉了。 regret

Jiékè:   Nà tài  kěxī  le!   Wǒ zài  nàr  chīguo jǐ  cì,   wèidao búcuò.
杰　克：那太可惜了！我在那儿吃过几次，味道不错。

Xiǎo Huáng:   Rúguǒ bù chāidiào nàxiē  jiù fángzi,   zěnme huì yǒu zhème piàoliang de
小　黄：如果不拆掉那些旧房子，怎么会有这么漂亮的

cǎodì  ne?
草地呢？

## 注释　Zhùshì　Notes

（一）一两年前

一两年 means 一年或者两年 (one or two years). Other examples: 七八个，十四五本，三四十块.

（二）那些旧房子早就拆掉了

掉, used as a complement, indicates that something is no longer there. Other examples: 我把那些书都卖掉了。/ 鸟儿被猫吃掉了。

# 12.3 Language Points

❀ The 被(bèi) Sentence

A sentence with the preposition 被 is called the 被 (bèi) sentence. Its structure is:

**Receiver of the action + 被 + doer of the action + V…**

E.g.（1）我的自行车被同学借走了。

（2）眼镜被他摔破了。

Sometimes the object of 被 needs not be included. For example:

（1）河里的鱼都被毒死了。

（2）那些旧房子早就被拆掉了。

In spoken language, 被 is often replaced by 叫 or 让. But 叫 or 让 must be followed by an object.

（1）我差点儿让汽车撞了。

（2）自行车叫人借走了。

The 被 sentence is different from the English passive voice. Most of the 被 sentences, especially in spoken Chinese, are used to refer to harm or hardship suffered by the subject, as shown by the above examples. Otherwise, the 被 sentence pattern is not required.

E.g.（1）火车票买到了吗?

（2）信已经写好了。

In the above two sentences 被 is not used.

⚙ Complete the following sentences using the verbs provided in the brackets. Add 被 to the sentences when necessary.

（1）早饭已经_____。（吃）

（2）我的电脑_____。（借）

（3）发票_____。（扔）

（4）电影票_____。（买）

（5）参观活动_____。（安排）

文化点　Wénhuàdiǎn　**Cultural notes**

When China first began its economic reform and opening-up, some regions pursued economic development without considering the environment. In recent years, environmental protection has become a hot button issue; people have become much more conscious of environmental protection and are devoting more attention to sustainable development. Many measures have been adopted to improve the environment, including afforestation (planting trees), prohibition of livestock grazing, reclaiming farmland, addressing problems concerning rivers and lakes, the establishment of protected area and allotting time for the rectification, or closure of factories with excessive pollution. The average area of green land per person in a city is also increasing yearly. However, environment protection is a great cause that requires the effort of government, business and each and every citizen. China still has much work to do to better its environment, but is now moving forward in a productive and positive manner.

# English Translation of the Texts

## Unit 1

### 1.1 I've raised birds before

| | |
|---|---|
| Jiang Shan: | Sir, this dog is very cute. |
| Old man: | Yes, it is. I've grown flowers and kept birds before, but I didn't like raising dogs. Since coming here, I've found that the people here are all fond of raising dogs, so now I raise dogs, too. |
| Jiang Shan: | I heard that in Chinese cities people are not allowed to raise dogs. Is that true? |
| Old man: | It was not permitted before, but now it is allowed. Some people like raising dogs; some like raising cats; some like raising birds; and some like raising fish. Do you like raising small animals too? |
| Jiang Shan: | I like small animals, but I don't raise small animals. |
| Old man: | Why not? Is it too troublesome? |
| Jiang Shan: | No, it's because I don't have the time, or the money. |

### 1.2 You must be very familiar with Beijing by now?

| | |
|---|---|
| Bai Xiaohong: | I hear that you're going to Beijing. Is it true? |
| Jack: | Yes, my company is sending me to Beijing on business. |
| Bai Xiaohong: | When are you leaving? |
| Jack: | Next Wednesday. |
| Bai Xiaohong: | You must be very familiar with Beijing by now? |
| Jack: | Of course. Look at these photos: this is the Palace Museum, this is the Summer Palace ... |
| Bai Xiaohong: | Have you ever climbed the Great Wall? |
| Jack: | "You're not a true man if you haven't conquered the Great Wall." How could I not climb the Great Wall? |
| Bai Xiaohong: | Have you been to any other cities? |
| Jack: | Shanghai, Xi'an, Chengdu ... I've been to all these cities. But there is still one place I haven't visited. |
| Bai Xiaohong: | Which place? |
| Jack: | Your home. |
| Bai Xiaohong: | You are welcome to visit. If you want to go, I can accompany you. But you have to pay |

for my plane ticket.

## Unit 2

### 2.1 She went to the hospital

| | |
|---|---|
| Teacher: | Has everybody come now? |
| Martin: | Wang Ying hasn't come yet. All of the others are here. |
| Teacher: | What happened to Wang Ying? |
| Martin: | I don't know. |
| Richie: | She lives in the dormitory. Every morning she eats breakfast in the dining hall. |
| Tanaka: | I think she might be having breakfast right now. |
| Jin Rongnan: | Maybe she's still sleeping. |
| Richie: | That's not possible. She has definitely gotten up. |
| Zhang Yuanyuan: | You're all wrong. Wang Ying has gone to the hospital. |
| Teacher: | What's wrong, is she sick? |
| Zhang Yuanyuan: | She feels a bit unwell. |

### 2.2 What did you eat for breakfast this morning?

| | |
|---|---|
| Wang Ying: | Doctor, my stomach aches. |
| Doctor: | Have you eaten anything unclean? |
| Wang Ying: | No, I haven't. |
| Doctor: | What did you have this morning? |
| Wang Ying: | A few slices of bread and a glass of milk .... But last night my friend treated us to dinner. We went to a restaurant near the campus. I ate many slices of raw fish. |
| Doctor: | Maybe the fish wasn't very fresh. You must take some medicine and .... |
| Wang Ying: | Excuse me ... |
| Doctor: | Calm down. I'm not finished talking yet. You must take some medicine and .... |
| Wang Ying: | Excuse me, where's the toilet? |

## Unit 3

### 3.1 They took the train here

| | |
|---|---|
| Gao Yifei: | Have you had breakfast? |
| Martin: | Not yet. Oh, could you lend me the new map that you bought yesterday? |
| Gao Yifei: | Yes. You can come to my room to get it. So, you're going out? |
| Martin: | After breakfast I'm going to accompany my parents to the National Museum. |
| Gao Yifei: | Your parents are here? |
| Martin: | Yes. |
| Gao Yifei: | When did they come? |
| Martin: | Last week. |
| Gao Yifei: | Did they come from Australia? |

| | |
|---|---|
| Martin: | No, first they went to Hong Kong and then to Beijing. Last week they came from Beijing by train. |
| Gao Yifei: | They haven't been to China before, have they? |
| Martin: | Yes, they have. This is already their sixth time. They are very interested in China's economy and culture. |
| Gao Yifei: | Oh, so they are two "Chinese experts." |

## 3.2 When did you borrow this book?

| | |
|---|---|
| Martin: | Is class over? |
| Wang Ying: | Yes, class is over. Where are you going? |
| Martin: | I'm going to the library to return a book. |
| Wang Ying: | Which book? |
| Martin: | A book written by an American. The name of the book is *How to Do Business with the Chinese*. Have you read it? |
| Wang Ying: | I've heard of it, but I've never read it; how is this book? |
| MaLi: | It's very good. You should read it, too. |
| Wang Ying: | Then don't return it. Let me read it. |
| Martin: | I'm afraid I can't. It's almost overdue. |
| Wang Ying: | When did you borrow this book? |
| Martin: | On the twentieth of last month. It's almost been one month, now. |
| Wang Ying: | Will they fine you if it's overdue? |
| Martin: | Of course. The library's rules stipulate that if an overdue book is not returned, you will be fined one yuan per day. |
| Wang Ying: | That's quite severe! Forget it; quickly go and return it. |

## Unit 4

### 4.1 She sings very well

| | |
|---|---|
| Martin: | You're dressed so handsomely today. |
| Richie: | I have a "foreign affairs activity" today. |
| Martin: | A "foreign affairs activity?" Are you meeting the Chinese President or the American President? |
| Richie: | Neither. I'm meeting my girlfriend's parents. This will be the first time I visit her home. |
| Martin: | Who's your girlfriend? |
| Richie: | You don't know? It's Xiao Zhang. |
| Martin: | Xiao Zhang? That especially cute, especially pretty girl? |
| Richie: | Yes. |
| Martin: | The girl whose singing is so pleasant to hear? |
| Richie: | Yes. |
| Martin: | The girl who dances so very beautifully? |

| Richie: | Right. |
|---|---|
| Martin: | She's your girlfriend? |
| Richie: | Yes. |
| Martin: | When did you meet each other? |
| Richie: | Last year. Do you have any more questions? |
| Martin: | No, I don't. (to himself) I'm too late! |
| Richie: | Too late? What do you mean? |

## 4.2 Martin is speaking Chinese especially fluently today

| Gao Yifei: | Happy birthday to you! |
|---|---|
| Xiao Zhang: | Thank you! |
| Martin: | This is my small gift for you. You were born in the Year of the Dragon; here's a jade dragon for you. |
| Xiao Zhang: | Oh, you're too nice! Thank you. Come on; let's eat the cake. |
| Martin: | (to Gao Yifei) Look, what's written on the cake? |
| Gao Yifei: | Aren't those the four characters for Happy Birthday? |
| Martin: | Oh, Happy Birthday.... Xiao Zhang, may you become prettier and prettier; and younger and younger. This year you're twenty, but next year you'll be eighteen. |
| Richie: | Martin is speaking Chinese especially fluently today. |
| Martin: | The more I drink, the more fluently I speak Chinese. |
| Xiao Zhang: | Ah, I understand; you mean— |
| Richie: | He wants another drink. |
| Martin: | OK. Come on, cheers! |

## Unit 5

### 5.1 It's not so hot in my hometown

| Richie: | It's really hot! |
|---|---|
| Gao Yifei: | Hot? |
| Richie: | Aren't you hot? |
| Gao Yifei: | It's not too bad. |
| Richie: | Did you hear today's weather report? |
| Gao Yifei: | I did. The high temperature will be 31 degrees Celsius. It's still not the hottest time yet. |
| Richie: | How is the weather in your hometown now? Is it as hot as here? |
| Gao Yifei: | It's even hotter than here. What about your hometown? |
| Richie: | It's not so hot. Summer in my hometown is much cooler than here. |
| Gao Yifei: | Then how about the winter? |
| Richie: | It's a bit colder than here. The low temperature is about minus eight degrees Celsius. |
| Gao Yifei: | It's that cold? |
| Richie: | But there's central heating in every room. It's very warm; not cold at all. |

## 5.2 Is the weather in your hometown the same as here?

| | |
|---|---|
| Wang Ying: | Is the weather in your hometown the same as here? |
| Gao Yifei: | About the same. It's very cold in winter, so we often go skiing. It's very hot in summer, so we often go swimming. What about your hometown? |
| Wang Ying: | The weather in my hometown is better than here. Our winters come later than here, and springs come earlier than here. |
| Gao Yifei: | That is to say, the winter is shorter. |
| Wang Ying: | And it's not so cold, either. |
| Gao Yifei: | What about the summer? |
| Wang Ying: | It's not so hot as it is here. |
| Gao Yifei: | That's a good place. |
| Wang Ying: | Yes, it is. Which season do you like best? |
| Gao Yifei: | Autumn. At that time, it doesn't rain much, and it's not windy. The weather is very nice. |
| Wang Ying: | I'm the same as you; I like autumn too. At that time, the maple leaves in my hometown all turn red. It's extremely beautiful. |

## Unit 6

### 6.1 There's a mountain on the north side of my house and a river on the south side

| | |
|---|---|
| Gao Yifei: | You're from the North, right? |
| Xiao Zhang: | Yes. My hometown is in the Northeast. |
| Gao Yifei: | Do you live in the city or in the countryside? |
| Xiao Zhang: | In the countryside. There's a mountain on the north side, and a river on the south side of my house. |
| Gao Yifei: | The air is fresh and the environment is very beautiful. It really sounds like a good place. |
| Xiao Zhang: | What's good about it? The transportation is not convenient at all. Is your home also in the countryside? |
| Gao Yifei: | My home is downtown. |
| Xiao Zhang: | It must be very lively there. |
| Gao Yifei: | Yes; to the east and west of my house, there are many shops, and several restaurants, too. In the front is a road, with heavy traffic from morning to night. |
| Xiao Zhang: | How great! |
| Gao Yifei: | What's great about it? It's so noisy! |

### 6.2 Is your home far from the sea?

| | |
|---|---|
| Li Xiaoyu: | Is your home in the east or the west? |
| Martin: | My home is in the east. |

| Li Xiaoyu: | Is your house big or not? |
| Martin: | Fairly big. My house is a two-storey building with a sitting room and a dining room on the first floor and bedrooms on the second. Behind the building is a garage. |
| Li Xiaoyu: | Does your house have a yard? |
| Martin: | It does. In front of my house there's a small yard. In the yard there are lots of trees and flowers. |
| Li Xiaoyu: | Is school far from your house? |
| Martin: | It's not too far. I drive to school every day. It takes about half an hour. |
| Li Xiaoyu: | Is your house far from the sea? |
| Martin: | It's not far; I often go to the seaside. After dinner, Anna and I go to the seaside for a walk. |
| Li Xiaoyu: | Your girlfriend likes to go to the beach, too? |
| Martin: | Girlfriend? Who is my girlfriend? |
| Li Xiaoyu: | Isn't Anna your girlfriend? |
| Martin: | No. Anna is my dog. |

## Unit 7

### 7.1 Practice Chinese for two hours each time

| Jack: | Hello. Let me first introduce myself. My name is Jack. I'm Canadian, and I'm glad to meet you. I have studied Chinese for half a year, but I can't speak it very well. |
| Chen Jing: | You speak pretty well. Let me introduce myself as well. I am a freshman majoring in English. My name is Chen Jing. I've been studying English for six years now, but my spoken English is not good. |
| Jack: | I've heard from friends that your Putonghua is exemplary and you speak English very fluently, too. |
| Chen Jing: | Thank you. My reading comprehension is passable, but not my listening and speaking skills; and my writing is poor. So I want to find a foreigner whose mother tongue is English to practice listening and speaking with me. |
| Jack: | That's great! I also want to practice my Chinese listening and speaking skills. How many times do you think we should meet each week? |
| Chen Jing: | Three times? |
| Jack: | OK. How long each time? |
| Chen Jing: | How about two hours of English practice and one hour of Chinese? |
| Jack: | Excuse me? I didn't hear you clearly. Did you say two hours of Chinese practice and one hour of English? That sounds great! |

### 7.2 OK. I'll say it once again

| Teacher: | First let's spend ten minutes practicing dictation with a few sentences. I will only read each sentence three times. |

| Martin: | Is it difficult? |
|---|---|
| Teacher: | It's very easy. Now let's begin. The first sentence: "Wǒmen qí zìxíngchē qù, wǒmen bú zuò qìchē qù." |
| Martin: | You are speaking too fast, sir. Could you please speak more slowly? |
| Teacher: | OK. I'll repeat it: "Wǒmen qí zìxíngchē qù, wǒmen bú zuò qìchē qù." |
| Martin: | What does it mean? I can't hear it clearly. "Wǒmen… qí zìxíngchē qù?" |
| Teacher: | Now, I'll say it one last time: "Wǒmen qí zìxíngchē qù, wǒmen bú zuò qìchē qù." |
| Martin: | It's too difficult. What is "zìxíngchē" ? |
| Teacher: | "zìxíngchē", we already learned it a while ago, didn't we? |
| Martin: | Sorry, I forgot it. Is that a kind of food? |
| Teacher: | You're not working hard enough! |
| Martin: | Sir, it's not that I'm not working hard. Last night I was drinking for over an hour, and I still feel muddled. |

## Unit 8

### 8.1 All the activities have already been scheduled

| Xiao Huang: | Is this Jack? |
|---|---|
| Jack: | Yes, it's me. |
| Xiao Huang: | This is Xiao Huang. I called you several times yesterday, but I couldn't get through. Is it confirmed that you'll be arriving next Tuesday? |
| Jack: | I'm afraid I won't be able to come. I have to postpone my journey until Wednesday. The train tickets for Tuesday have all been sold out. |
| Xiao Huang: | But Wednesday's activities have already been scheduled. |
| Jack: | What are the activities? |
| Xiao Huang: | We will visit the finance and trade center in the morning, the markets in the afternoon and in the evening our boss will host a banquet in your honor, which the managers of several international trading companies will also attend. |
| Jack: | Then I won't take the train; I'll take a plane instead. I'll buy a plane ticket for next Tuesday immediately. |
| Xiao Huang: | Please text me a message after you get the ticket to let me know your flight number. We'll meet you at the airport. |
| Jack: | No problem. Thank you. |
| Xiao Huang: | OK, it's settled then. Goodbye! |

### 8.2 We both fell down

| Policeman: | What's happened here? |
|---|---|
| Pedestrian: | He knocked me down. |
| Policeman: | Didn't you see her crossing the road when you were riding your bike? |
| Richie: | I couldn't see clearly because of the raincoat I'm wearing. |

| | |
|---|---|
| Pedestrian: | He was riding very fast and holding something in his right hand. |
| Policeman: | Didn't you see him approaching on his bike when you were crossing the road? |
| Pedestrian: | I couldn't see clearly because I was holding an umbrella. |
| Policeman: | What then? |
| Richie and Pedestrian: | We both fell down. |
| Richie: | My bike got broken. |
| Pedestrian: | My glasses got broken. |
| Policeman: | Are you injured? |
| Pedestrian: | I don't know. My back hurts a little. |
| Policeman: | Listen here; (to Richie) you should take her to the hospital to get her back examined, (to the pedestrian) and after that, you should take him to repair his bike. |
| Pedestrian: | But I have to get to work. |
| Richie: | And I have to get to school. |
| Policeman: | Then you should ... |
| Richie and Pedestrian: | Say goodbye! |

## Unit 9

### 9.1 Can we take this contract back for a look?

| | |
|---|---|
| Wang Ying: | Do you have an apartment for rent? |
| Mrs. Qian: | Yes. If you want to rent it, you can move in right now. |
| Wang Ying: | Which floor is it on? |
| Mrs. Qian: | The sixth floor. Want to go upstairs and have a look? |
| Wang Ying: | Is there an elevator? |
| Mrs. Qian: | No, there isn't. You have to walk upstairs. |
| Zhang Yuanyuan: | It's very tiring to walk upstairs and downstairs every day! |
| Mrs. Qian: | It doesn't matter; you'll get some exercise that way! (arriving at the sixth floor) Come in, please. |
| Zhang Yuanyuan: | How much is the rent per month? |
| Mrs. Qian: | Three thousand yuan. |
| Wang Ying: | That's too expensive! |
| Mrs. Qian: | It isn't expensive at all. You see, there are two big rooms in this apartment. There is a TV, a refrigerator, a washing machine and a telephone. |
| Zhang Yuanyuan: | Do we have to pay a deposit? |
| Mrs. Qian: | You must pay a three-thousand-yuan deposit, which will be returned to you when you move out. Here is the contract. |
| Wang Ying: | We'll go back and think about it; we'll call you tomorrow. Can we take this contract back for a look? |
| Mrs. Qian: | Yes, of course. I'll be waiting for your call tomorrow. |

## 9.2 Please buy and install it soon

Zhang Yuanyuan: It's such a hot day, and there is no air conditioning in the room. It's really annoying!

Wang Ying: Yes. It is too much! Let's call Mrs. Qian and see what she says.

(Dials the telephone) Is that Mrs. Qian?

Mrs. Qian: Yes. What can I do for you?

Wang Ying: It has already been several days since the air-conditioner was removed. Is it fixed?

Mrs. Qian: Sorry. It hasn't been fixed yet. The technician said the air-conditioner is too old; there's no way to fix it.

Wang Ying: Then what should we do?

Mrs. Qian: Then …

Zhang Yuanyuan: You'll spend some money buying a new one.

Mrs. Qian: (takes the telephone) It looks like I have to buy a new one.

Zhang Yuanyuan: Then please buy it and install it soon.

Mrs. Qian: I'll buy it as soon as I have some free time.

Zhang Yuanyuan: When will you be free? We'll die from the heat!

Mrs. Qian: Oh, I'm so sorry .... I'll go to the electrical appliance store to have a look this afternoon. If I can buy one then, I'll get the shop to deliver it at once.

## Unit 10

### 10.1 Can you get the tickets?

Gao Yifei: There is a Beijing Opera show tonight. Let's go watch it together, all right?

Wang Ying: I'm afraid that I don't understand it.

Gao Yifei: It doesn't matter. It's a kung fu show. Even if you don't understand the words, you can definitely understand it just by watching the action.

Wang Ying: Are the actors famous?

Gao Yifei: I can't recall their names, but according to the newspaper, they are all very famous.

Wang Ying: Can you get the tickets?

Gao Yifei: No problem, I can definitely get them.

Wang Ying: Front row seats would be best. I have poor eyesight; I won't be able to see clearly if I sit in the back.

Gao Yifei: Don't worry about it.

Wang Ying: All right then, when do we leave?

Gao Yifei: The Opera begins at seven p.m.; let's leave at a quarter past six.

Wang Ying: Can we make it there in half an hour?

Gao Yifei: Sure. Let's go by taxi; we'll get there in a quarter of an hour if there are no traffic jams.

### 10.2 Too tired to even speak

Li Xiaoyu: I can't go on.

| | |
|---|---|
| Tanaka: | Look, Xiaoyu is too tired even to speak. |
| Gao Yifei: | Xiaoyu can't climb any further. Let's take a rest. |
| Li Xiaoyu: | Let me drink some water. How far is it to the mountaintop? |
| Wang Ying: | We've only climbed halfway up. There's still halfway left to go. |
| Li Xiaoyu: | It looks like I won't make it to the top of the mountain. You go up; I'll wait for you at the foot of the mountain. |
| Martin: | You ordinarily get too little exercise. |
| Li Xiaoyu: | It's not that I get too little exercise; it's just that I have so many things to deal with that I can never finish them all. How would I find the time to exercise? |
| Martin: | It's not that you don't have the time; you're just too lazy. |
| Wang Ying: | You can't just think of work; make sure that you also get your rest. |
| Tanaka: | I suggest that you go jogging every morning from now on. |
| Gao Yifei: | I'll teach you Taiji Boxing. |
| Li Xiaoyu: | You should go now. Let me rest here quietly for a while. |

## Unit 11

### 11.1 Where did you put your wallet?

| | |
|---|---|
| Martin: | Oh no, where's my wallet? |
| Mother: | Is it lost? |
| Martin: | Impossible. When we got off the car just now, I paid the money. At that time my wallet was still there. |
| Mother: | Where did you put your wallet after paying? |
| Martin: | Oh, how terrible! I left the wallet on the seat. |
| Father: | How could you do that! |
| Mother: | Now what do we do? |
| Father: | Call the taxi company at once. Do you still remember the plate number? |
| Martin: | I can't remember it at all. |
| Father: | Did you get the receipt? |
| Martin: | I thought the receipt was useless, so I threw it into the garbage can. |
| Mother: | How much money was there in your wallet? |
| Martin: | About five hundred US dollars. |
| Mother: | You've given these five hundred US dollars to the driver. |

### 11.2 I'll bring the wallet over to you immediately

| | |
|---|---|
| Martin: | Hello, who's this? |
| Driver: | This is the taxi driver. This morning you took my taxi; did you leave something in my car? |
| Martin: | Oh yes, we left a wallet in the car. |
| Driver: | I'll bring it over to you immediately. |

| Martin: | Oh! Thank you so much! How did you find our wallet? |
| Driver: | A passenger saw the wallet and gave it to me. |
| Martin: | What a good person! But how did you get our phone number? |
| Driver: | We checked the contents of the wallet, and found a piece of paper on which had the name and address of the hotel you're staying at. I called the hotel and the front desk transferred me to your room. |
| Martin: | That was really very kind of you. |
| Driver: | That's all right. You must have been very worried. |
| Martin: | Yes, for sure. Just now my mother was yelling at me, because there are passports and other documents in the wallet; it would have been troublesome if I had lost them. |

## Unit 12

### 12.1 The bicycle was missing

| Wang Ying: | I had such bad luck today! |
| Martin: | What's the matter? |
| Wang Ying: | As soon as I got up this morning and opened my computer, I found that there was something wrong with it: no files exist. |
| Martin: | Did your computer break down? |
| Wang Ying: | My computers must have a virus. |
| Martin: | Didn't you install anti-virus software? |
| Wang Ying: | Yes, I did, but it was useless. |
| Martin: | That's impossible. What will you do now? |
| Wang Ying: | I have a friend who can help me. However, I rode so fast on the way to his house that I neglected the traffic lights and was nearly hit by a car. |
| Martin: | You were so anxious. |
| Wang Ying: | When I arrived at his home and opened the computer, I found my files reappeared. He told me that something might be wrong with the hardware. |
| Martin: | That's fine since no files were lost. |
| Wang Ying: | But when I walked out his home, I found my bike was missing. |
| Martin: | Your bike was missing? |
| Wang Ying: | Yes, exactly. |
| Martin: | You are really unlucky! |

### 12.2 All the fish in the river were killed by poison

| Jack: | I remember when I came here several years ago, the river was seriously polluted. All the fish in the river were killed by poison. |
| Xiao Huang: | Now the river has become clean. Look, there are fish in the river again. |
| Jack: | Great changes have taken place. If I didn't come for a visit, I wouldn't believe it. These trees were planted one or two years ago, weren't they? |

| | |
|---|---|
| Xiao Huang: | Yes. How did you know? |
| Jack: | When I came last time, this road was under repair and all the trees on both sides of the road had been cut down. |
| Xiao Huang: | Now the government stipulates that no one can just carelessly cut down trees. |
| Jack: | Those lawns are not bad, either. —Hey, I seem to remember there used to be some small restaurants selling all kinds of refreshments, over there. |
| Xiao Huang: | Those old houses were knocked down a long time ago. |
| Jack: | That's such a pity. I've eaten there several times before; the dishes tasted pretty good. |
| Xiao Huang: | If those old houses hadn't been knocked down, how could there be these beautiful meadows now? |

# Supplementary Text

## Zài Hūnlǐ Shang
## 在 婚礼 上
### At the Wedding

**Words and expressions**

| | | | | |
|---|---|---|---|---|
| 1. | 教堂 | ( N. ) | jiàotáng | church |
| 2. | 举行 | ( V. ) | jǔxíng | hold; carry out |
| 3. | 婚礼 | ( N. ) | hūnlǐ | wedding |
| 4. | 入乡随俗 | | rùxiāng-suísú | "When in Rome, do as the Romans do." |
| 5. | 新娘 | ( N. ) | xīnniáng | bride |
| 6. | 毕业 | ( V. ) | bìyè | graduate |
| 7. | 新郎 | ( N. ) | xīnláng | bridegroom |
| 8. | 同事 | ( N. ) | tóngshì | colleague |
| 9. | 俩 | | liǎ | two |
| 10. | 谈恋爱 | | tán liàn'ài | be in love (courting) |
| 11. | 成 | ( V. ) | chéng | succeed |
| 12. | 同意 | ( V. ) | tóngyì | agree |
| 13. | 怕 | ( V. ) | pà | be afraid of |
| 14. | 过不惯 | | guò bu guàn | cannot get used to |
| 15. | 原因 | ( N. ) | yuányīn | reason |
| 16. | 虎 | ( N. ) | hǔ | tiger |
| 17. | 吵架 | ( V.O.) | chǎojià | argue, quarrel |

| 18. | 岂有此理 | | qǐyǒucǐlǐ | it's outrageous |
|---|---|---|---|---|
| 19. | 后来 | (TW) | hòulái | later |
| 20. | 脾气 | (N.) | píqi | temper |
| 21. | 认真 | (Adj.) | rènzhēn | serious |
| 22. | 感情 | (N.) | gǎnqíng | feelings |
| 23. | 确实 | (Adj.) | quèshí | true, real, indeed |
| 24. | 反对 | (V.) | fǎnduì | oppose; be against |
| 25. | 醉 | (V.) | zuì | be drunk |
| 26. | 交杯酒 | (N.) | jiāobēijiǔ | the nuptial cup of wine |

(One year later, Martin starts to work in a joint-venture company. Another half year passes, and he becomes engaged to his colleague, Li Xiaoyu, a Chinese girl. Jack, Bai Xiaohong, and Jiang Shan have flown all the way from the other side of the ocean to attend their wedding. Martin's classmates from Chinese class and his Chinese friends have also come.)

Jiāng Shān: Tāmen zěnme méi qù jiàotáng jǔxíng hūnlǐ?
江　山：他们怎么没去教堂举行婚礼？

Jīn Róngnán: Rùxiāng-suísú ma.
金容南：入乡随俗嘛。

Lǐqí: Xīnniáng tǐng piàoliang de. Nǐ rènshi ma?
里　奇：新娘挺漂亮的。你认识吗？

Gāo Yìfēi: Rènshi, jiànguo jǐ cì miàn. Tā xìng Lǐ, yě shì wǒmen xuéxiào
高一飞：认识，见过几次面。她姓李，也是我们学校

bìyè de.
毕业的。

Lǐqí: Shì ma? Wǒ yìdiǎnr yě bù zhīdào.
里　奇：是吗？我一点儿也不知道。

Bái Xiǎohóng: Tīngshuō xīnláng, xīnniáng shì tóngshì?
白小红：听说新郎、新娘是同事？

Tiánzhōng: Duì, tāmen liǎ zài tóng yí gè gōngsī gōngzuò, tán liàn'ài tánle
田　中：对，他们俩在同一个公司工作，谈恋爱谈了

yì nián duō le.
一年多了。

白小红：听说 最后差点儿没 谈成？
*Bái Xiǎohóng: Tīngshuō zuìhòu chàdiǎnr méi tánchéng?*

田 中：是啊。小李的母亲听说了这件事以后，不太同意。
*Tiánzhōng: Shì a. Xiǎo Lǐ de mǔqīn tīngshuōle zhè jiàn shì yǐhòu, bú tài tóngyì.*

张 园园：为什么？
*Zhāng Yuányuan: Wèi shénme?*

江 山：那还 用 说？把女儿交给一个 "老外"，能 放心吗？
*Jiāng Shān: Nà hái yòng shuō? Bǎ nǚ'ér jiāo gěi yí gè "lǎo wài", néng fàngxīn ma?*

张 园园：有什么不放心的？
*Zhāng Yuányuan: Yǒu shénme bú fàngxīn de?*

田 中：是有点儿不放心。怕小李跟一个外国人在一起
过不惯。
*Tiánzhōng: Shì yǒudiǎnr bú fàngxīn. Pà Xiǎo Lǐ gēn yí gè wàiguórén zài yìqǐ guò bu guàn.*

张 园园：已经谈了一年多了，还会有什么问题？
*Zhāng Yuányuan: Yǐjīng tánle yì nián duō le, hái huì yǒu shénme wèntí?*

田 中：还有一个原因，小李比他大两岁。
*Tiánzhōng: Hái yǒu yí gè yuányīn, Xiǎo Lǐ bǐ tā dà liǎng suì.*

王 英：大 两 岁有什么关系？
*Wáng Yīng: Dà liǎng suì yǒu shénme guānxi?*

田 中：你知道吗？小李属虎，马丁 属龙。
*Tiánzhōng: Nǐ zhīdào ma? Xiǎo Lǐ shǔ hǔ, Mǎdīng shǔ lóng.*

王 英：我还是不明白。
*Wáng Yīng: Wǒ háishi bù míngbai.*

田 中：你学了这么 长 时间的汉语了，连 这 也不懂？
*Tiánzhōng: Nǐ xuéle zhème cháng shíjiān de Hànyǔ le, lián zhè yě bù dǒng?*

王 英：老师没教过。
*Wáng Yīng: Lǎoshī méi jiāoguo.*

田 中：老人 说，要是一个属虎，一个属龙，以后会
吵架的。
*Tiánzhōng: Lǎorén shuō, yàoshi yí gè shǔ hǔ, yí gè shǔ lóng, yǐhòu huì chǎojià de.*

杰 克：岂有此理！那后来呢？
*Jiékè: Qǐyǒucǐlǐ! Nà hòulái ne?*

田 中：见了几次面以后，他们发现，马丁汉语说得很
*Tiánzhōng: Jiànle jǐ cì miàn yǐhòu, tāmen fāxiàn, Mǎdīng Hànyǔ shuō de hěn*

liúlì, píqi yě hěn hǎo, zuò shì yě fēicháng rènzhēn, Mǎdīng
流利，脾气也很好，做事也非常认真，马丁

gēn Xiǎo Lǐ de gǎnqíng yě quèshí fēicháng hǎo. Suǒyǐ, tā
跟 小李的感情也确实非常 好。所以，她

mǔqīn jiù bù fǎnduì le.
母亲就不反对了。

...
……

Jīn Róngnán: Kàn, xīnláng, xīnniáng zǒu guòlai le.
金容南：看，新郎、新娘 走过来了。

Jiāng Shān: Mǎdīng, jīntiān děi duō hē jǐ bēi ya.
江 山：马丁，今天得多喝几杯呀。

Mǎdīng: Bù xíng, wǒ hē bu xià le, wǒ jiù yào hēzuì le.
马 丁：不行，我喝不下了，我就要喝醉了。

Gāo Yìfēi: Nǐmen liǎ hái méi hē jiāobēijiǔ ne!
高一飞：你们俩还没喝交杯酒呢！

Mǎdīng: Hǎo ba, zuìhòu yì bēi. Lái, wǒmen yìqǐ gānbēi!
马 丁：好吧，最后一杯。来，我们一起干杯！

Gāo Yìfēi: Bù xíng, bù xíng. Zhè shì jiāobēijiǔ, nǐ zhǐ néng gēn xīnniáng hē.
高一飞：不行，不行。这是交杯酒，你只能跟新娘喝。

Mǎdīng: Shì ma?
马 丁：是吗？

Gāo Yìfēi: Xiǎoyǔ zhīdào zěnme hē, ràng tā jiāo nǐ ba.
高一飞：小雨知道怎么喝，让她教你吧。

## 文化点 Wénhuàdiǎn Cultural notes

There are three major forms of wedding ceremony found around the world: the ritual wedding, the religious wedding, and the civil wedding. The ancient Chinese practiced a very complicated ritual wedding. Today the marriage customs are much simpler. The main point is applying to the local authorities for a marriage certificate. After the marriage certificate is issued, people will then generally distribute "happy candies" (xǐtáng) to relatives, friends, and colleagues; then there is a wedding ceremony.

There are three kinds of modern wedding ceremonies:

(1) The wedding banquet (xǐyàn): relatives, friends, and others are invited for dinner and wedding toasts. A simple ceremony is performed during the banquet.

(2) The travel wedding (lǚxíng jiéhūn): the bride and groom go off on a trip together, and when they return, they are considered to be married. Some will have a simple ceremony before they leave on the trip.

(3) The group wedding (jítǐ jiéhūn): this kind of wedding is organized by institutions or public groups. Several pairs or dozens of pairs of brides and grooms take part in one wedding ceremony together.

# Two Chinese Folk Songs

## Mòlìhuā
## 茉莉花

（江苏民歌）

## Jasmine Flower

(Jiangsu folk song)

好 一朵茉莉 花， 好一朵茉莉

好 一朵茉莉 花， 好一朵茉莉

好 一朵茉莉 花， 好一朵茉莉

花， 满园 花 草 香也香不过它；

花， 满园 花 草 雪也白不过它；

花， 满园 花 草 比也比不过它；

我 有心 采 一朵 戴，又怕 看花 人

我 有心 采 一朵 戴，又怕 旁人

我 有心 采 一朵 戴，又怕 来年

将　我　　骂。

笑　　　话。

不　发　　芽。　　　我　有　心　采　一　朵

戴，又　怕　来　年　不　发　　芽。

**Introduction**

The tune "Jasmine Flower" derives from a song which has been popular ever since the Qing Dynasty (1616–1911) in the regions north and south of the Yangtze River. The song was originally called, "Scholar Zhang Teases Maiden Yingying." Scholar Zhang and Maiden Cui Yingying are the protagonists of the famous Yuan Dynasty drama, "Romance of the West Chamber." In their pursuit of freedom in marriage, they smash the bounds of tradition, surmount all obstacles and win true love in the end. The original song had more than ten sections, but the most popular one is the tune "Jasmine Flower" from the lower Yangtze basin. In the song, the pretty, fragrant jasmine flower is praised as a metaphor for the bitter-sweetness of love, with the contradictory sentiments of desiring the flower, yet being fearful of its keeper. As early as the late eighteenth century, this song had spread to the West. It was used by the Italian composer Puccini in his opera "Turandot." In 1979, it was recommended to UNESCO as one of the songs to be promoted in Asian countries. "Jasmine Flower" has become part of the repertoire for foreign musical groups visiting China.

What a pretty jasmine flower! What a pretty jasmine flower! None of the flowers in the garden are more fragrant than it. I'd like to pick it to wear, but I'm afraid its keeper will scold me.

What a pretty jasmine flower! What a pretty jasmine flower! Its pure white blossom outshines the snow. I'd like to pick it to wear, but I'm afraid people will laugh at me.

What a pretty jasmine flower! What a pretty jasmine flower! None of the garden's blooming flowers can compare with it. I'd like to pick it to wear, but I'm afraid it won't bud next year. I'd like to pick it to wear, but I'm afraid it won't bud next year.

# Cǎoyuán Qínggē
# 草原　　情歌

（青海民歌）

# Love Song on the Grasslands

(Qinghai folk song)

徐缓　优美抒情地

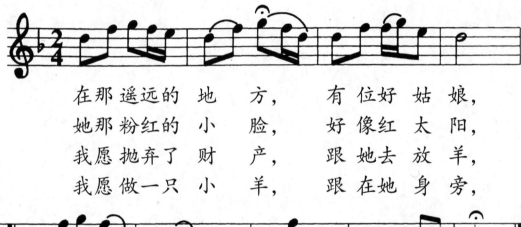

在那 遥远的　地　方，　　有 位 好 姑　娘，
她那 粉红的　小　脸，　　好 像 红 太　阳，
我愿 抛弃了　财　产，　　跟 她 去 放　羊，
我愿 做一只　小　羊，　　跟 在 她 身　旁，

人们 走过了 她的　毡房，都要回头 留恋地张　望。
她那 美丽　动人的眼睛，好像晚上 明媚的月　亮。
每天 看着那 粉红的笑脸 和那美丽 金边的衣　裳。
我愿 她拿着 细细的皮鞭，不断轻轻 打在我身　上。

**Introduction**

"Love Song on the Grasslands" is a traditional folk song popular in Qinghai. The song depicts the fascinating picture of green prairies, a flock of white sheep, a beautiful shepherd girl and a herdsman. It praises the shepherd girl's beautiful appearance, using lovely similes such as: "Her little, pink face looks like the red sun, and her beautiful and charming eyes look like the radiant and enchanting moon." The affectionate young herdsman shows his passion for the girl: "I'd give up all I have, and tend the sheep with her," "I'd like to become a little lamb beside her, and I'd wish her to keep tapping me gently with her tiny whip." The young man's protestations of love are passionate and sincere, lively and delightful, and profound and witty. This folk song is melodious, sweet, and strongly appealing. It is much beloved, and has become part of many singers' regular repertoire.

In a faraway place, there is a pretty girl. Passing by her tent, people crane their necks and look back with yearning.

Her little, pink face looks like the red sun, and her beautiful and charming eyes look like the radiant and enchanting moon.

I'd like to give up all I have, and tend sheep with her. Every day I'd look at that pink smiling face and that beautiful dress with golden lace.

I'd like to become a little lamb beside her, and I'd wish her to keep tapping me gently with her tiny whip.

# 词语索引 Index of Vocabulary

The number after the word represents the ordinal number of the text.

200. 觉得 juéde / 11.1
201. 卡片 kǎpiàn / 11.2
202. 开 kāi / 6.2
203. 开始 kāishǐ / 7.2
204. 砍 kǎn / 12.2
205. 考试 kǎoshì / 7.2
206. 可能 kěnéng / 2.1
207. 可惜 kěxī / 12.2
208. 刻钟 kèzhōng / 7.2
209. 客厅 kètīng / 6.2
210. 肯定 kěndìng / 2.1
211. 空调 kōngtiáo / 9.2
212. 空气 kōngqì / 6.1
213. 恐怕 kǒngpà / 3.2
214. 口袋 kǒudài / 11.1
215. 口语 kǒuyǔ / 7.1
216. 快 kuài / 3.2
217. 快乐 kuàilè / 4.2
218. 款 kuǎn / 3.2
219. 垃圾 lājī / 11.1
220. 垃圾箱 lājīxiāng / 11.1
221. 懒 lǎn / 10.2
222. 老家 lǎojiā / 6.1
223. 老人家 lǎorénjia / 1.1
224. 累 lèi / 9.1
225. 冷 lěng / 5.1
226. 礼物 lǐwù / 4.2
227. 历史 lìshǐ / 3.1
228. 厉害 lìhai / 3.2
229. 连……都／也…… lián…dōu／yě… / 10.2
230. 练习 liànxí / 7.1
231. 凉快 liángkuai / 5.1
232. 了 le / 1.1
233. 领导 lǐngdǎo / 8.1
234. 流利 liúlì / 4.2
235. 楼 lóu / 6.2

236. 楼 lóu / 9.1
237. 麻烦 máfan / 1.1
238. 马上 mǎshàng / 8.1
239. 骂 mà / 11.2
240. 嘛 ma / 9.2
241. 慢 màn / 7.2
242. 猫 māo / 1.1
243. 贸易 màoyì / 8.1
244. 没（有）méi (yǒu) / 2.1
245. 没用 méiyòng / 11.1
246. 美 měi / 5.2
247. 美元 měiyuán / 11.1
248. 面包 miànbāo / 2.2
249. 名片 míngpiàn / 11.2
250. 明白 míngbai / 4.2
251. 母亲 mǔqīn / 3.1
252. 母语 mǔyǔ / 7.1
253. 拿 ná / 3.1
254. 哪些 nǎxiē / 1.2
255. 那么 nàme / 3.2
256. 那些 nàxiē / 1.2
257. 南边（南面）nánbian (nánmiàn) / 6.1
258. 南方 nánfāng / 6.1
259. 难 nán / 7.2
260. 年 nián / 7.1
261. 年级 niánjí / 7.1
262. 年轻 niánqīng / 4.2
263. 鸟儿 niǎor / 1.1
264. 牛奶 niúnǎi / 2.2
265. 农村 nóngcūn / 6.1
266. 努力 nǔlì / 7.2
267. 暖和 nuǎnhuo / 5.1
268. 暖气 nuǎnqì / 5.1
269. 爬 pá / 10.2
270. 拍照 pāizhào / 1.2
271. 跑 pǎo / 10.2

272. 跑步 pǎobù / 10.2
273. 陪 péi / 1.2
274. 片 piàn / 2.2
275. 票 piào / 1.2
276. 平时 píngshí / 10.2
277. 破 pò / 8.2
278. 普通话 pǔtōnghuà / 7.1
279. 其他 qítā / 11.2
280. 起 qǐ / 2.1
281. 起床 qǐchuáng / 2.1
282. 签 qiān / 9.1
283. 钱包 qiánbāo / 11.1
284. 清 qīng / 12.2
285. 清楚 qīngchu / 7.1
286. 晴天 qíngtiān / 5.2
287. 请客 qǐngkè / 2.2
288. 秋天 qiūtiān / 5.1
289. 去年 qùnián / 4.1
290. 热 rè / 5.1
291. 热闹 rènao / 6.1
292. 扔 rēng / 11.1
293. 容易 róngyì / 7.2
294. 如果 rúguǒ / 9.2
295. 软件 ruǎnjiàn / 12.1
296. 散步 sànbù / 6.2
297. 杀 shā / 12.1
298. 杀毒 shādú / 12.1
299. 山顶 shāndǐng / 10.2
300. 伤 shāng / 8.2
301. 上班 shàngbān / 8.2
302. 身体 shēntǐ / 2.1
303. 生 shēng / 2.2
304. 生气 shēngqì / 9.2
305. 生日 shēngrì / 4.2
306. 生肖 shēngxiào / 4.2
307. 生意 shēngyi / 3.2
308. 生鱼片 shēngyúpiàn / 2.2

# 语法项目索引 Index of Grammatical Items

# 功能项目索引 Index of Functional Items

**35.** **[Restating]**

也就是说，冬天比较短。      5

**36.** **[Starting a conversation]**

老人家，这只小狗真可爱。      1

听说，你要去北京了？      1

**37.** **[Suggestion]**

你也应该看看。      3

来，咱们吃蛋糕吧。      4

上去看看吧？      9

咱们休息休息吧。      10

我建议你以后每天早上出去跑步。      10

**38.** **[Supposition]**

大概还在睡觉呢。      2

可能生鱼片不太新鲜。      2

他们以前没来过中国吧？      3

那儿一定很热闹。      6

**39.** **[Surprise]**

哇，这么厉害！      3

女朋友？谁是我女朋友？      6

是吗？有这样的事儿！      12

**40.** **[Sympathy]**

你真倒霉。      12

**41.** **[Talking about past actions]**

昨天晚上朋友请客，我们去了学校附近
的一个饭店，我吃了很多生鱼片。      2

**42.** **[Talking about past experience]**

你登过长城吗？      1

**43.** **[Urge]**

你快点儿去还吧。      3

**44.** **[Worry]**

我恐怕听不懂吧。      10

责任编辑：史文华
英文编辑：张　乐　吴爱俊
封面设计：Daniel Gutierrez
插　　图：笑　龙

**图书在版编目（CIP）数据**

《当代中文》课本 . 2：汉英对照 / 吴中伟主编 . — 修订本 . — 北京：华语教学出版社，
2014.7

ISBN 978-7-5138-0731-9

Ⅰ . ①当… Ⅱ . ①吴… Ⅲ . ①汉语 – 对外汉语教学 – 教材 Ⅳ . ① H195.4

中国版本图书馆 CIP 数据核字 (2014) 第 155000 号

《当代中文》修订版

课本

2

主编　吴中伟

*

© 孔子学院总部 / 国家汉办

华语教学出版社有限责任公司出版

（中国北京百万庄大街 24 号　邮政编码 100037）

电话：(86)10-68320585, 68997826

传真：(86)10-68997826, 68326333

网址：www.sinolingua.com.cn

电子信箱：hyjx@sinolingua.com.cn

北京密兴印刷有限公司印刷

2003 年（16 开）第 1 版

2015 年（16 开）修订版

2020 年修订版第 6 次印刷

（汉英）

ISBN 978-7-5138-0731-9

定价：79.00 元